Girl Reel

memoir

Girl Reel

bonnie j. morris

a lesbian
remembers
growing up
at the movies

coffee house press

2000

copyright © 2000 Bonnie J. Morris
author photograph Myra J. Morris
book + cover design Kelly N. Kofron
cover + back cover photographs © PhotoDisc

Coffee House Press is an independent nonprofit literary publisher supported in part by a grant provided by the Minnesota State Arts Board, through an appropriation by the Minnesota State Legislature, and in part by a grant from the National Endowment for the Arts. Significant support has also been provided by The McKnight Foundation; Elmer and Eleanor Andersen Foundation; Jerome Foundation; the Target Foundation; General Mills Foundation; St. Paul Companies; Butler Family Foundation; Honeywell Foundation; Star Tribune Foundation; James R. Thorpe Foundation; Lila Wallace Reader's Digest Fund; Pentair, Inc.; the Helen L. Kuehn Fund of The Minneapolis Foundation; the law firm of Schwegman, Lundberg, Woessner & Kluth, P.A.; and many individual donors. To you and our many readers across the country, we send our thanks for your continuing support.

Coffee House Press books are available to the trade through our primary distributor, Consortium Book Sales, 1045 Westgate Drive, St. Paul, MN 55114. For personal orders, catalogs, or other information, write to: Coffee House Press, 27 North 4th Street, Suite 400, Minneapolis, MN 55401.
www.coffeehousepress.org

Library of Congress CIP Data

Morris, Bonnie J.
  Girl Reel : memoir / Bonnie J. Morris.
    p.   cm.
  ISBN 1-5689-094-2 (alk. paper)
  I. Title.
  PSXXX.XXX 2000
  811'.54—dc21

00-XXXXXX
                 CIP

10 9 8 7 6 5 4 3 2 1
first printing / first edition
Printed in Canada

for Jennifer Rosse and Camille Smith
for Jeanette Buck
for my brother, John
and for certain beloved movie theaters we have known:

The Key   The Ritz

Grauman's Chinese   The Chincoteague Island Roxy

The Jenifer   The Paris

The Carthay Circle   The Lakewood Center I and II

The Carolina   The Tammuz

The K.B. Baronet   The Circle Theater

The Biograph   The Embassy

The Northgate Plaza I and II   The MacArthur

The Yorktown

contents

i **introduction** when we were hollywood brats

Reel 1 girlhood

1 Silence Please

7 How I Spent My Allowance

23 My Father's Tears

29 The Ram Man

Reel 2 adolescence

The K.B. Baronet 35

Function in Disaster 45

The Girl-Gang Movies 55

Steven Spielberg's Cousin 63

Julia: Love between Women as a Slap in the Face 71

Coming Out at The Rocky Horror Picture Show 81

Reel 3 higher education

93 Myra and Mr. Sulu

101 Another Night at the Tammuz

111 Yentl: Women Who Want Something More

121 Sappho Goes Hollywood: How We Looked to American Moviegoers

131 Batman: A Few Notes on Looksism

139 A Tribute to Director Maria Maggenti

149 Working with Jodie . . . and Working with Jeanette

165 epilogue a ticket stub

Girl Reel

Roger Morris, age 12, and his sister Patricia Morris, age 6

introduction
when we were hollywood brats

1

In Southern California it is known as The Industry.
The movie studios will eat you alive—or make you
rich; lie to you—or grant you the fame and celebrity
you have sought all your days. No one growing up
in West L.A., not my father and his sister, nor my
mother, nor myself, remained untouched by the
lure and influence of Hollywood, which oozed
gelatinously from the executive honeycombs of
offices, studios, premieres, and deals. Yet all four of
us, at different times, said NO to Hollywood, to
being packaged as images for sale.

My father and his sister were movie extras, studio
children in the Great Depression and the forties,
with salaries earned from their extraordinary good

i

looks and the hovering possibility of futures "under contract." They were groomed for fame by my grandmother, Evelyn Morris, a woman with a war-absent husband and great ambitions for her handsome children.

Tap dance and acting classes, modeling sessions, and glossy 8 x 10 portfolios haunted my father's childhood. He began his career as the infant model for the Adohr Milk campaign: little Roger Morris, the "Adohr-able" baby in the Los Angeles papers. At three he tap-danced and played the ukelele in an act called "Roger Morris and his Swing Band"; he went on to take prizes as the Most Hollywood Type Boy in studio modeling competitions and worked on movie sets with the Little Rascals, Ginger Rogers, and Mickey Rooney, among others. He remembers the great Disney premieres of the late thirties and early forties, when the Seven Dwarves paraded down his street, and studio executives led a deer representing Bambi past his house on Del Valle Drive.

Roger's little sister Patty, who appeared on the cover of *Good Housekeeping* as a toddler model, was sent to school each day so carefully outfitted and coiffed that teachers wrote despairing letters to my grandmother requesting that Patricia come to school dressed like an ordinary child. Together, Roger and Pat appeared in any number of forgettable motion pictures as children, but in their last mutual gig they won roles in the best science fiction picture of their youth, *The Day the Earth Stood Still*. Even now, in 1999, I can walk into a repertory movie theater, or an art cinema/coffeehouse like the Beehive in Pittsburgh, and see a cult revival screening of *The Day the Earth Stood Still*. There on the big screen is my aunt's famous close-up as the terrified little girl at the start of the story, and there is my father in his high school club jacket, pointing up at and running away from the spaceship.

They both quit the business. They quit when they reached adolescence, rather than joining the Screen Extras Guild and paying union dues; their father, the Major, had come home from World War II denouncing unions and ridiculing union organizer John L. Lewis. More personally, they quit the industry for other adolescent reasons. Groped by a very popular and "wholesome" actor behind one studio when she was still a kid, my aunt had her reasons. Taunted as a pretty actor-boy when neighborhood standards of masculinity called for all cool and hip teenage dudes to join a club or a gang, my father had his reasons. It was a bitter disappointment for their ambitious mother when they quit, right around the beginning of a new era in Hollywood, called television.

Neither Pat nor Roger, today, enjoy having their photographs taken. Neither of them enjoy talking about their Hollywood childhoods. At best they will respond with expletives when I ask for adjectives. Prying a movie set story from my father and aunt, when I am lucky enough to corner them together, is akin to opening a can of tuna with a pair of tweezers. Eventually, you will get in, but only a tiny portion will be rendered unto you.

The one story my father tells from time to time sums up the panic he felt when his Hollywood brat life destroyed a hallmark of regular boyhood: his paper route. He was on his way to an important modeling session, a professional photography shoot in a canyon with Lassie or some other movie dog, and suddenly he realized his appointment would make him late delivering the evening papers. When he expressed a ten-year-old's anxiety about the time, describing his paper route obligations to the studio agent sitting behind him in the chauffered car, the agent looked at him and said, "You're not going to make it."

At this point my father describes the sinking feeling he experienced as he realized he could not get out of the car and go back, that the limousine to fame was literally speeding him faster and faster away from neighborhood life and cares. When he tells this story I can picture his striped shirt against the luxurious car upholstery, and, later, his fear of the huge, unfamiliar dog he was made to pose with for hours while the Hearst papers went undelivered. My father tells me this one story because he does not want me to think fame and glamour are of higher rank than small, serious joys. I keep the professional glossy of my father and the dog over my writing desk, to remind me.

I knew nothing of my family's Hollywood past until I was fairly big, and the stories I've been able to extract from the tuna can would only feed a sparrow.

My mother's contact with The Industry was different. Also a beauty, she nonetheless grew up with a marginal self-image, painfully aware of being the daughter of Jewish immigrants in a blond, debutante beach culture. Her greatest desire was not fame but anonymity, the ability to pass as Gentile; born in Brooklyn and moving to Hollywood at three, she reenacted the journey of so many first-generation American Jews in the film industry, Santa Monica beachcombers with New York accents. In my mother's home lived her old grandmother from Warsaw, who spoke Yiddish rather than English and screamed "shit" as a cooking instruction. My mother went to school with my father's sister Pat and lived in awe of Pat's Gentile good looks, movie outfits, blue eyes. In those pre-Streisand years no one promoted Jewish good looks in Hollywood culture, and actual Jews in The Industry had their ethnicity masked by Gentile pseudonyms.

After high school my mother went to work for a Hollywood legend, the Academy Award-winning actress Greer Garson, who lived in seclusion in Bel Air. As personal secretary to Miss Garson my mother handled correspondence and ran errands, and had tea with the orange-haired older woman every day on the veranda. "Why aren't you in the pictures?" Miss Garson demanded of my mother. "You're young and beautiful." She was regally unaware of my mother's Jewish self-consciousness, though by then my mother had taken to calling herself Jean rather than Myra, and had put a blonde streak in her black hair.

In fact, my rebellious glamorous mother had terrible stage fright and not the remotest interest in acting. She laughed politely when Tom Laughlin, who later made the controversial film *Billy Jack*, came up to her on the UCLA campus and offered to cast her in the pivotal role of the schoolteacher. She blushed modestly when Greer Garson insisted that beauty would send her far. My mother was, by then, in love with my father, and didn't desire to be sent anywhere. When she gave notice at Miss Garson's, announcing she was leaving her position to get married, the aging actress sent my parents a silver shot glass as a wedding gift. To this day, my father measures his vodka in this glass.

My father, my aunt, and my mother each said NO to The Industry before they were twenty, but many of their friends and classmates said YES. To read their old yearbooks is to see today's celebrities as pimply adolescents. There is Dustin Hoffman at sixteen, on the tennis squad at L.A. High, where he was known as "Dusty"; there is George Takei—*Star Trek*'s "Mr. Sulu"—in student government with my mom. And there were others. If I marvel at seeing my father on-screen, he and my mother marvel at seeing expressionless nerds from their high school hallways transformed into movie poster gods, emblazoned on lunch boxes and toys.

So it was in the air, this thing. All of us were Hollywood material in someone's eyes, Hollywood brats even when we declined The Industry's tentacles. Good looks meant that strangers on the street assumed you were working. Good looks were family status, currency in a town which turned on faces. Each successive generation had to be even more Hollywood-beautiful, in exponential narcissism.

People talked because my father married a Jewish girl, because he went against the code of marrying blonder, of cultivating Hollywood eugenics. But when I was born to this mixed couple I emerged with formula good looks, as Hollywood-Gentile in appearance as any agent's dreams. Strangers stopped my mother in Westwood to say "You ought to put that pretty baby in the movies." Soon I was taken to sit for 8 x 10 glossy photographs at Reed's of Hollywood, where the photographer informed my mother that my dislike of bright flash bulbs indicated pathological insecurity. I was not even two years old.

I found my core of security, my loud feminist voice, the minute I arrived at that first Hollywood audition and decided I could say NO instead of YES to strange men. Thus my own wee career with The Industry went no further than the casting director telling me I had to wear makeup just like mommy, and my outright refusal. While I was inside, giving a two-year-old's equivalent of a raised middle finger to the director and makeup man, my mother overheard another parent interrogate her auditioning baby: "Did you give them your big personality smile?" "Oy," my mother declared, and took me home. I only discovered the large, unused portfolio of expensive toddler 8 x 10 glossies of myself when I was in junior high, earning movie money by cleaning out our basement.

And so I grew up ordinary. Ah; but not normal. I was too smart to be normal, and, eventually, I also found out that I was queer.

2

After my 8 x 10 glossies went into a drawer and I took up ordinary childhood, I began going to the movies with my parents. The first picture I saw in a theater was *Born Free,* which impressed me deeply at age five, because it seemed permissable for men to cry at this movie. I heard my father, a man with a tight rein on his emotions, stand in our driveway afterward and tell a neighbor that we had all cried at this movie. It was then that I realized that a movie was not something you saw, but a mere part of what happened to you at the movies, which could mean anything. Hmm, I thought.

To be sure, the sixties were prime movie time if you were a schoolkid, because Disney churned out film after film, not just for movie theaters but for *The Wonderful World of Disney* on NBC every Sunday night. I saw *Mary Poppins* four times, *The Love Bug* four times, and the various animated classics—*Snow White, Dumbo, Peter Pan,* ad infinitum, all over L.A. I saw many of my childhood movies at Grauman's Chinese Theater (now Mann's), with the handprints in cement outside; and at least once a year went to Disneyland itself, where movie characters each had their own ride. I went to drive-in movies with my parents, falling asleep in the backseat on a pincushion of popcorn while my baby brother drooled on the gearshift knob up front; I had a collection of children's records based entirely on movie scores: *The Sound of Music, The Jungle Book, The Wizard of Oz.* On a regular basis, we saw movie stars in restaurants or on the beach; if you went trick-or-treating at Bob Hope's house, whispered a girl I met at summer camp, he gave out silver dollars.

We drove past the enormous and secretive studios on an almost daily basis, as Nebraskans drive past corn.

Every child knew that the best movie of all, even if you really LOVED *Mary Poppins* or *The Jungle Book,* was of course *The Wizard of Oz;* but the strange thing about this was that it never came to a real movie theater anymore. Instead it was on TV one night a year, and that night was third to Christmas Eve and Halloween in schoolkid anticipation. Merely mentioning it to my contemporaries, even now, brings a gush of nostalgia. "Oh, my God, yeah," burble my friends Tracy and Reed. "On the night of *The Wizard of Oz* you had your bath first and then you put on your p.j.s and then you got to eat dinner in front of the television with a blanket." This assumes one had a color TV at home: we did not, so I rotated through the homes of various friends and relatives who did, on that special night each year.

Because L.A. was in no way a small or safe town in the late sixties, I was nearly ten before I walked to a movie theater alone with a friend. I went with Brenda Moskwitz, the toughest girl on the playground at Clover Avenue Elementary, and we saw—ah!—*The Wizard of Oz.* We wanted to see how it measured up on the big screen, when at last it came to a real theater we could walk to, unescorted. But by then we found we had become hardened to Hollywood mush; when Judy Garland began saying her tearful farewell to the Scarecrow, Brenda stomped out and I followed her back to the schoolyard. It was important to Brenda to always look tough and never willingly suffer mush; she declared to me that she hated Hollywood and that The Industry wasn't so great. She was the first friend I went to the movies with alone; later, she became beautiful, got a Hollywood agent, modeled for The Industry; and died at thirty-two, the first friend I lost to breast cancer.

A lot changed when I was nine; for one thing, I became moody and frustrated, because I had outgrown Disney and dolls and was reading at a level about ten years ahead of my peers. What I wanted now was to watch *To Kill a Mockingbird,* over and over, until I felt I understood it; my parents threw other literary classics at me to stall my obsession with the story of a rape trial, but there was no turning back. I read the book and saw the movie and thought I understood. I was, I thought, finished with childhood.

The second change was that we left L.A. for good. My father had gone back to school, received his graduate degree, and accepted a job in Durham, North Carolina, three time zones and infinite worlds away from Hollywood movie studios and the Pacific Ocean.

So having lived my first decade as a Hollywood brat, I came of age on the East Coast: five years as a Southerner in Durham, and the rest in Washington, DC, the three cities of my personal identity an impossibly convoluted triangle, and the peculiar Americanism of each place continually at odds with my emerging lesbian sensibilities in adolescence.

In every place that is not quite home one may find sanctuary in a movie theater, as I often did growing up; but no film ever pays homage to real girlhood, which remains a secret to America. We are our own biographers, for The Industry has concluded there is no money to be made in girlhood. I am still talking back to the director I denounced at two, the one who believed even an Aryan-looking baby girl needed makeup; I am speaking now as a witness from my seat in the front of the theater. You have to know who we are by now, us queer girls. We grew up in front of you, our lives a private girl reel. Some of us spent that girlhood at the movies.

3

This is a collection of movie stories: by which I mean recollections of events, images, turning points generated by specific moviegoing experiences, and, of course, specific movies. Some of my stories begin in a movie theater and others take their time getting there, but all have in common the catalyst of a movie outing as a chunk of formative girl identity.

Do you, too, remember your favorite movie house in the old neighborhood? The double feature you saw over and over again with your first gang? The flasher you encountered behind the theater that day; the nightmares from scary film classics; the fantasies about screen heroines? Do you remember seeing your first "lesbian movie," and wondering why it was so dreadful? Did you, too, come out at the movies?

In America, we are all shaped and shifted by moviegoing, and at an early age find ourselves in conversation with that big screen, anxiously patching ourselves against the silhouettes of movie stereotypes to see if we'll ever fit Hollywood's notion of glamorous. We all know that "the gaze" of the camera is male, and that there are far more roles reserved for men both in front of and behind the Hollywood camera; and that movies about

childhood escapades or pranks will be about boyhood pranks—
as though no girl ever skipped off to look for hidden treasure.

But girls as well as boys and grown-ups go to the movies and
grow up there, and I was no exception. Although moviegoing
greatly influenced my life, I should state here at the beginning
that I did not become a film critic. Instead, my Ph.D. is in
women's history, the end result of a lifelong interest in memory
and its symbols. As an academic woman I'm an oddity in
money-conscious America, for we are no longer a nation of
readers or writers. We have long been a media nation in the
making, and since the era of talking pictures a substantial per-
centage of our population has used moviegoing for emotional
expression, rather than keeping a journal or—heaven forbid—
crying and talking with a loved one in the privacy of bed.

Desperate for emotional outlets, we go to the movies as an
excuse to hold hands, to weep copiously, to feel a vicarious and
"safe" ethnic experience, to be sexually aroused, to grieve. We
go to get out of the house when family members are fighting,
or we go because we like to eat popcorn and Jordan Almonds
in the dark. We go to have a broad spectrum of feelings flashing in front of us in a vertical therapy session, while we, knees
up and bodies open as though to receive lovemaking, are the
passive horizontal. Popcorn box between our knees, we dip
our hands repeatedly between our own legs, the act of recre-
ational feeding a mimicry of self-loving, self-stimulation. Surrounded by complete strangers, we can snicker, gasp, and sob,
knowing that our personal reactions to carefully budgeted
stimuli will never be a matter of public record because no one
is watching us. In this group experience, this audience experience, there is safety for emotional display. The actual film is
almost irrelevant.

And perhaps most comforting of all is the universal factor in
moviegoing: everyone goes, old, young, parent, child, male,
female. Leaving aside, for the moment, our American past of

racially segregated movie theaters, and our complex present of X-rated films, we acknowledge that most moviegoing experiences are open to a diverse public society. At *Apollo 13* I saw two ten-year-old boys seated next to a middle-aged Congresswoman next to punk high school lovers next to a group of gay men next to a homeless woman. Everyone is here, but no one is talking to or looking at one another. That is the irony of The Industry's success: the most American thing you can do is go to the movies, which in turn are the most American and influential product we export; and the nature of the moviegoing experience is being completely alone in a democratically demographic crowd: our bittersweet American characteristic, our individualism. You have to find it for yourself, this conversation; as Lily Tomlin said it, "We're all in this alone."

Reel 1

girlhood

Silence Please

I took my first film studies course at age eleven when I began attending the notorious Carolina Friends School in Durham, North Carolina. This private alternative school is still a shining planet in Durham's educational orbit; still loyal to the philosophy of the Society of Friends, or Quakers. In 1972, however, the school's "experimental" structure and informal student-teacher hierarchy elicited mixed reactions from the population of Durham. Conservative folk clicked their tongues and swore that no child learned anything out at that wild Commie school in the woods. Liberals, in despair over the state of the local public school system, where daily prayer and arbitrary corporal punishment were still enforced in blithe disregard of

1

federal law, felt a magnetic tug toward the long Carolina Friends School waiting list. My parents got me in.

We began each day with silent meditation, called "settling in." The school was very young then, filled with ebullient long-haired kids and ebullient long-haired teachers; in a nation bitterly divided over Vietnam, Friends took an actively antiwar stance and peace studies was a part of the curriculum. Far from learning nothing, most of us in the middle school were intellectually abuzz, riveted by national politics and global issues. The glory of a Friends School education was that of course we studied traditional subjects such as writing and mathematics, but we were also free to choose electives like Animal Behavior, Women's Studies, Solar Energy, Folk Dance—and, in 1972, the History of Silent Film.

The film studies course was simply called Silence Please. Students were expected to show up and watch respectfully. The host was a teacher named Greg Garneau, who initially planned to offer Silence Please only for upper school students at Friends. However, at the time, the upper school had yet to be built, and the high school students were meeting for classes in any spare room or free space, including the musty middle school building. This was how I was able to sneak into every screening of Silence Please that year.

Greg believed in cultural literacy for young people, and screened what he understood to be the great silent pictures of early cinema: *Nosferatu, The Battleship Potemkin, Phantom of the Opera*. We, clandestine eleven-year-olds, admitted probationally to Greg's screenings, sat cross-legged on the gray industrial school carpeting and tried not to scream. Whenever we shrieked at the horror on parade—Nosferatu's predatory grimace, the Phantom's self-hating "accursed ugliness," Sergei Eisenstein's famous baby carriage crashing down the Odessa Steps (from which my own great-grandmother Rivka fled a pogrom)—Greg would simply lift his moustache from behind the projector and purr, ever superior, "Silence, please."

By day, I preened with the honor of being permitted to study world cinema with Greg. By night, I wrestled with the problem of nightmares I did not care to have.

I would not let myself dream of Nosferatu's face. Could my own willfulness prevent his intrusion in my sleep? How much discipline did I, at eleven, have over what frightened me?

At dinner, over the hamburgers and tater tots, I casually asked my parents about dream life. "What makes us dream about weird or scary things?" I took a drink of milk from my favorite red plastic cup, which was shaped like a cowgirl boot. "I mean, things we totally don't want to dream about?"

My father explained about the human subconscious. "You are exposed to an image, a comment, an event, that is filed away in your brain even after you think you've forgotten all about it. In sleep, these subconscious incidents or images come back. Thus, something you might have been exposed to even once can linger, troubling you in a way you won't be aware of until you sleep. Dreams pick from what is filed at the back of the mind. They are your unfinished business."

I decided then and there that the key to my problem was simple: control. I had to organize my own brain into a protective, self-serving bulwark against the wily subconscious. If one only dreamed about fearful images from the subconscious, maybe I could avoid nightmares by keeping all scary thoughts conscious: actively, blatantly at the front of my mind right before I went to sleep at night. Everything scary had to be right out there where I could keep an eye on it, rather than impractically "forgotten," which seemed to guarantee a later reappearance.

I tested this theory. Curled in my top bunk, I brought out the faces of every scary person I did not want to encounter in

3

my dreams. There was Nosferatu, poised to suck at my young neck. There was the Phantom, his mask jerked off to reveal a frightening visage. There were the broken and bleeding faces of Odessa, the woman's eyeglasses smashed into her face. Nosferatu, again. The Phantom, again. When I had allowed this mental tape loop of intimidating pictures to play several times, I figured I was safe from nightmares—my fears now manipulated into conscious, not subconscious, location.

It really worked! I never had nightmares, and the few "bad" dreams I did have as I grew older never involved horror movies. My personal brand of inoculation against ghosts from the subconscious pleased me. I learned that I could control my mind, if not my body, which was unwillingly steamrolling into puberty at an alarming pace.

At eleven, these one-on-one psychoduels with the misunderstood monsters of cinema had everything to do with my own changing appearance. Like Nosferatu, my teeth were enormous and hanging, and my overbite had begun to distort my face.

I had grown sharp teeth at the incredibly early age of three months, forcing my punctured young mother to switch me from breast-feeding to a sterile bottle before I was even as old as a quarterly bank statement. I spent the next seven years rapturously sucking my thumb, as my father refused to permit me a pacifier; he felt they looked unbecoming on intelligent children. Now he was literally paying the price for his aesthetic preferences: I wore expensive new braces on my teeth. In time, the braces would cure my overbite and allow my face to resume its intended shape. But for a year or more, when I was eleven and twelve, part of my bedtime routine involved becoming a suffering monster myself.

Promptly at eight P.M. each evening the grease-spattered clock on the kitchen stove reminded me that it was time to attach my "night brace," a phrase I cannot write without feeling, to this day, that slow ache in my back molars and the half-circle of pain sliding around my upper jaw. For as long as I had braces I spent half of my life, the twelve hours from eight P.M. to eight A.M., harnessed into this contraption, a thick wire which slid into slots on my back braces and was hooked around my neck in a stretch pad. All night long, unable to sleep on my side, I drooled uncomfortably as the brace reined my teeth in and shifted my facial structure to the required standard. The brace left strange indentations in my neck, like Frankenstein's bolt marks. Certainly, I knew this was temporary, best for me in the long run, a privilege. Fashionable, even; normative, healthy. For-my-own-good. Preventative medicine: the orthodontist at Duke University Medical Center showed me the file of photographs of spooky women with all the facial malformities that I could develop if I didn't obey my regimen of braces. On my way to and from the orthodontist's office I also had to walk through the plastic surgery ward, where I had additional glimpses of scary people: faces I had to incorporate into my nightly exercise program of what not to dream about.

Going directly from Silence Please class to my orthodontist appointments that year, I realized that anyone could be the Phantom of the Opera: me, the malformed girl in the medical photofile whose family couldn't afford to get her teeth fixed, the kid awaiting plastic surgery; anyone could be a vampire, unable to go out in daylight where people would stare at you and run in horror; if I didn't have braces my teeth would all fall out, the orthodontist warned; I would be the unvampire, incapable of biting. I hated being shown photographs of what I could turn out like if I cheated on my night brace. One time after Dr. Quinn showed me the file of bad patients and hopeless cases, all of whom ended up ugly, I wore a pair of sharp Halloween fangs to my next orthodontist appointment.

I was a monster in training. Every morning I stripped off my night brace and wiped my chin, letting the throb in my molars subside to an ache, as my face gradually resumed its daily comfort like a reinflating lung. Adults insisted I'd have a beautiful smile Later On, but this Later On business troubled me to no end, as I knew it also included breasts, lunar bleeding, and unpredictable acne. Worse, I would end up like Betty and Veronica in Archie comic books, distinguishable from my peers only by hair color and cretinous beaus. To stave off later ugliness I had to be scary now, the point being to look perfect by adolescence, when good looks ruled the earth.

I began to experiment with being a monster by day, by attracting simultaneous sympathy and revulsion, like the lonely Phantom and the unloved Nosferatu. Instead of sleeping in my night brace, I wore it to school to see how people would react. I wore it to the shopping center. And I wore it to the movies, until I tired of being unable to eat candy. Then I reverted to sleeping in the brace and, instead, went to the movies with my arm in a sling or my leg artificially bloodied or whatever mild monstrosity came to mind: enough to experience what it felt like to be treated differently, to be treated as a body, not as an intelligent mind.

I went to the movies wearing a black Chinese wig. I went to the movies and spoke in a foreign accent. I told people I was a Polish refugee, a Spanish refugee, a German refugee. I pretended I could not speak at all. I limped, I lied about my age, I wore a phony cast on my arm; I did everything I could think of to get people to look at someone they might feel uncomfortable looking at. I took my night brace off and washed it in the movie theater bathroom sink. I waited for someone to say something offensive, patronizing, prejudiced, rude. And then I turned and glared, and leaned into their faces and said, "Silence, please."

How I Spent My Allowance

During the years we lived in Durham, my brother
Johnny and I received our weekly allowance on
Friday nights. This was an important ritual because
our parents were not very affluent people; as kids
we never had much money in our pockets. We got
our allowance on Friday and it was gone by Sunday; the rest of the week we mowed lawns, baby-
sat, hunted for deposit bottles, set up lemonade
stands, biked to Duke Gardens and stole coins
from the wishing pool; until Friday came again.

Our daddy, Roger, affectionately called Big
Weeg, came home from work on a Kawasaki motorcycle, the smell of tobacco haunting his clothes. In
his tangerine-colored helmet he resembled a cool
lean lollipop. He threw down his keys as we ran to

greet him and stood peeling off his government work clothes, magically turning into weekend man. He opened up his wallet and handed me a dollar. I would spend it all the next day.

I spent my allowance on many things, but I always ended up at the movies: first the Yorktown Theater on 15-501 and later the Center I and II at Lakewood Shopping Center, the Carolina Theater downtown, and the Northgate Plaza. Most of these movie houses were within biking distance, and I was old enough to spend Saturdays on my own. But how I got to the movies was never a straight line between, say, our yard and the Yorktown. It was more of a complicated Saturday dance, of teetering between play and seriousness in my allowance-spending choices. After all, I was eleven years old; and I remember what it was like to be eleven years old on Saturday morning in 1972.

1

On Saturday morning I woke up in my top bunk and looked at my cat poster for a while. I took a moment before getting up to see if I could still get into the full lotus position without using my hands, still bend my thumbs back to my wrists, still roll my tongue, still wiggle my ears, cross my eyes, write left-handed and upside down and backward. These things were important.

My brother Johnny had been up since six A.M. watching monster movies on the small black-and-white television in our family den. *Sunrise Theatre,* the first broadcast of Saturday morning, showcased the continuum of Japanese monsters: Godzilla, Mothra, Ghidrah, Gemara. We were all on a first-name basis. Johnny and I soon realized we could write a Japanese monster screenplay ourselves, as there was almost no variation: you needed a small brave schoolboy, his cowering and inept adolescent sister, a professor in a lab, and one other guy whose job it was to say "Ho! A strange creature!" and "Masao, get the professor!"

This took us up until eight A.M. or so, when our formal TV watching began. To be sure, Saturday morning children's television in the early seventies was an embarassment even to us. After *Sunrise Theatre* came *The Uncle Paul Show*, a local experiment featuring a scary woman who implored us through stiff lips, "JESUS wants to be YOUR best friend." I was already cynical about this, having heard rumors that Uncle Paul, attending a party in our own neighborhood, sat at the piano with a young woman in his lap and strong drink at hand.

Then followed dozens of cartoon programs starring teenage rock groups and garage bands, with "songs" serving as soundtrack filler during chase scenes. Whether these series revolved around actual performing artists, like the Jackson Five, or grafted musical hobbies onto fictitious characters, one simply couldn't avoid the implication that all red-blooded American kids had rock-touring gigs and never attended school. This message was reinforced by any of the following programs: *The Archies, The Hardy Boys, Josie and the Pussycats, The Osmonds, The Jackson Five, The Banana Splits, The Monkees, The Groovie Ghoulies,* and so on. The excruciating music usually turned out to be a product kids had to buy, like the Archies' hit "Sugar Sugar," which came on the back of the Honeycomb cereal box. Yes, everybody was famous on Saturday morning, and presumably the characters' gigs helped pay for their endless adventures by motorcar, plane, and chopper. The message that instant fame came without school or talent or effort did a great deal to prepare us for the inarticulate MTV world we would create as adults. But we didn't know that then, our mouths full of breakfast cereal, our eyes glazing over.

I tuned in to this mess because a few racial breakthroughs sufficed to make the cartoon world interesting. *The Chan Clan,* for instance, was the only all-Asian cartoon program ever produced, and even the voices were dubbed by Asian kids—except for the butch tomboy girl, whose lines were read by Jodie Foster. *Josie and the Pussycats in Outer Space* featured a resourceful black female engineer named Valerie, who piloted the girl band into space with competence and focus. As a sop to racial tolerance, when Val spoke her mind you never heard a laugh track. She was a genuine feminist role model, far more so than Velma on *Scooby Doo,* whose genius for solving mysteries was cancelled out by the pointed misogyny of her homeliness.

On Saturday morning the real world intruded at regular intervals in the form of public service commercials, which seemed hatched out of hell and served as morbid counterpoints to the rest of television's sugary banter. There were pointed anti-smoking ads that no kid would ever forget. There were antidrug ads featuring death, heartbreak, screaming wind-up toys. There were antipollution ads, the famous single tear rolling down the face of the Native American chief. There were haunting depictions of haggard, freaked-out men returning from Vietnam, with the slogan "Don't forget. Hire the vet." There were all the Metropolitan Life commercials, which showed kids having medical emergencies, struggling with learning disabilities, being rushed to hospitals with attacks and diseases. There was the shot of a grade school classroom with the announcer hissing "ONE OF THESE CHILDREN HAS EPILEPSY; CAN YOU TELL WHICH ONE?" And, finally, there was an eerie public service announcement for religious unity, with a full range of human pain and anguish in quick cutaway shots: a lonely elderly woman with Parkinson's disease, a profoundly retarded girl, then the atomic bomb exploding. Each sequence was followed by the thunderous question "Why?" and answered with "GOD IS HOPE; GOD IS LOVE."

My brother and I sat through these commercials in silence, occasionally exchanging controlled, swift glances. It was important not to cringe, not to cry, not to react with any visible emotion in front of one another.

By noon I was out the door, bagel in hand, ready to spend my allowance. Before wheeling my mother's old bicycle up the driveway I turned a few obligatory cartwheels—I had vowed to cartwheel once a day for the rest of my life, so that I'd never lose this important skill. I could cartwheel well enough, walk on stilts, walk on my hands both on lawn and underwater; I had won swimming ribbons at the Durham YMCA. Yet my parents insisted that I needed to play more, to go outside and run around instead of reading, reading, reading. Thus every Saturday I biked for miles around Durham, in spirited willingness to go beyond bookwormism; and inevitably, I ended up at the movies.

2

But first I biked to Eagle Stamp and Coin. This was far, so I entertained myself en route by inventing stories in which I was this or that kind of heroine. (I wondered, at the time, licking my braces against the wind, if I would still talk to myself in this way as a grown-up.) My biking fantasies drew on the motif of prepubescent fame from Saturday morning television: I held admiring documentary interviews with myself at each stoplight on Chapel Hill Road. I was the youngest writer ever to win a journalism prize; I accepted an Academy Award by thanking my parents and my creative writing teacher; I was an escaped Armenian princess returning to liberate her homeland; I was the youngest cousin of the Beatles and went on tour with them; I came from a poor Iberian fishing village and led a campaign to give girls equal rights.

By the time I reached Eagle Stamp and Coin I was exhausted from pedaling and fame. The kindly older woman who managed the establishment loved and trusted me, and let me browse for hours; I returned her affection by spending much of my allowance here. Stamps seemed a tunnel to the beyond —perhaps the only way a child could understand political change. One could own history in the form of commemorative stamps from countries that were no longer politically independent.

Latvia, Lithuania, Estonia, Azerbaijan; long before the stunning renationalization of these countries in the wake of Soviet collapse, I learned their prewar names, examined their languages in the warmth of the magnifying glass. The trick, for a girl on a fixed allowance, was to choose the item of greatest political significance per penny. But I debated whether it was even permissible for a Jewish girl to collect Third Reich stamps —canceled with a swastika, these had possibly accompanied the writs of deportation for my own ancestors.

It was too much. At a certain point I would scram, back to kidhood, to permitted ignorance, to the mild follies of Saturday, away from the enforced genocides and assimilations whispered by thin paper stamps.

Before I went to the Saturday movie matinee I stopped at the Kwik Pik to buy Wacky Packages, which were only a dime and barely counted as spending.

The Kwik Pik, over on 751 before it was renamed Academy Road, offered a fine assortment of kid stuff. They sold magic tricks, superballs, curly drinking straws that mothers hated because they couldn't be cleaned, Silly Putty, wax lips, clik-claks, and jacks. They sold slurpees that turned one's lips and tongue a reckless artificial aqua, beef jerky and Slim Jims in cellophane, jars of Mary Janes and Atomic Fireballs and speckled jawbreakers, drumstick ice cream pocked with cardboardy walnut sprinkles, and, because it was the South, giant hot pickles and pig's feet. But I was a well-trained Jewish daughter and forbidden to eat junk food between meals; I walked beneath a healthy umbrella of guilt, and rarely bought snacks.

Right by the candy counter, new comic books twirled like cartoon ballerinas in their round rack, inevitably offering Archie and Jughead, Millie the Model, Dennis the Menace, Little Lulu, and the multiple male superheroes girls seldom differentiated. For the stout of heart there was also a sampling of "scary" comic literature, the supernatural tales and mysteries, the Hurricane Man and the Man with the Flaming Scar, omen figures who always turned up as a warning before every impending disaster. No thanks. Brrr.

What I liked were the really fringe comic heroes, the non-comformists, the mavericks, the kid characters, as opposed to adult figures or high-breasted teenagers. These were all published by Harvey Comics, with the jester jack-in-the-box logo. Take a bow, Harvey; you offered a lineup of truly spunky oddballs: Little Dot, Little Lotta, Richie Rich, and the tantalizing Hot Stuff—an actual spawn-of-Satan devil child with a pitchfork, whose comic series was noticeably absent in our Bible Belt convenience store.

For me, Little Lotta was a pinwheel of feminist hope. A strong, friendly blonde girl whose primary quality was her enormous bulk, Lotta never apologized for being big. Instead she literally threw her weight around to save the day, sitting on, or occasionally landing on, her male foes. The series blew to smithereens unkind stereotypes about passive or slow-thinking fat kids, as Lotta did not lack for action or inspiration. In one spectacular story line well ahead of its time, Lotta's doctor put her on diet pills, which severely interfered with her sleeping and working habits and caused dangerous mood swings. Lotta's family conceded that she was far healthier without drugs, and threw out her medication. What a boon to the generations of chubby girls born after Judy Garland!

Regrettably, the eleven-year-old girl in 1972 had only two options in convenience store literature. There were the comic books. And then there were the fan magazines: *Spec, Sixteen, Tiger Beat, Partridge Family Magazine,* and so on; you were supposed to choose a lover among Donny Osmond, David Cassidy, Bobby Sherman, or Michael Jackson. I chose Donny. His teeth gleamed from countless pinups taped to my bedroom wall. I spent many hours on the phone with my best friend, organizing all ten Osmonds and Jacksons into our personal order of preference (Donny, Jay, Marlon, Michael, Merrill, Jermaine, Tito, Alan, Jackie, Wayne). I also had a personal subscription to *Partridge Family Magazine,* which I let lapse with utter relief. It came with a companion booklet, *1001 FACTS ABOUT THE PARTRIDGE FAMILY*—in most instances more than one wanted to know. "Danny Bonaduce loves to give people electric shocks!"

We who were about to get breasts found these magazines a mixed blessing. On the one hand, they certainly urged young women to mold ourselves into fashion-addicted groupies, pop consumers whose developing brains focused on Donny's appendectomy scar rather than the war in Vietnam. On the other hand, some fanzines did not shy from issues of the day, addressing head-on those white supremacists who objected to seeing the Jackson Five alongside the Osmonds. When an irate racist mom wrote in to one fanzine and complained "You make the Jacksons out to be as good as white people," the editors replied "We do not condone prejudice and were shocked by your letter," and the millions of eleven-year-old white girls who read this exchange were forced to think about racism.

There is a photo of me at eleven, sitting on our battered living room couch, knock-kneed and eating sunflower seeds, wearing moccasins and nappy polyester shorts from the Sears Catalog—and reading *Sixteen.* I would cut out the slick posters of teen idols and trade them with my best friend, who couldn't go out to buy fanzines herself because she was grounded for something like two years. We found most pop idols literally interchangeable and enjoyed making composite faces from different celebrity features: Donny's nose, Bobby's eyes, David's chin. Eventually I threw out all my Osmond scrapbooks and gave my back issues of *Sixteen* to the born-again girls down the block, who secretly erected a shrine to the icon David Cassidy at the foot of their beds.

3

I climbed back on my bike, having resisted temptation to spend any more money; I was finally on my way to the movies. It was the first year that I was allowed to go to movies alone, and I was having a hell of a good time forging a private relationship between myself and the big screen; between myself and the theaters of Durham.

This was the fresh tributary of my political life, this movie-choosing; for I discovered that I had tastes and preferences, reactions and fears, favorite performers and despised performers, and strong opinions on the restriction of young people by film rating. Any box office I approached forced me to choose an identity: child or adult, in ticket price, and here adult status began at twelve or thirteen, in bar mitzvah fashion. With my wee allowance I found it thrifty to pass for under twelve, even when I was twelve and, later, thirteen, squatting in my worn sneakers to look young. Yet many theater managers in Durham were of the opinion that an under-twelve should only see movies with a G rating. This was before GP became PG and PG-13, and I knew I had a legal right to see anything rated GP, but I constantly experienced the following exchange at the box office:

"Hi. One child, please."

"Are you under twelve? You're surely a big eleven, for a girl. Gettin' boobies. Don't you go throwing that ticket stub down, we just vacuumed the lobby. Now you know this picture's rated

GP. It's got four-letter words and I don't know what all. Your mama know about that? She gonna like that?"

I'd hand over seventy-five cents and glare at the box office lady with the painted V-shaped eyebrows; insist, "It's my allowance."

"All right, go on in, sweet Jesus Lord. I wouldn't let my daughter see this trash, that's all. A hippie movie. You sure you have your parents' permission?"

"My parents are hippies," I'd say gleefully, and smile with all my braces.

For G-rated movies and no hassles you biked to the Yorktown. The Yorktown, down on 15-501 near the Lions Club, catered to young people and during the summer showed kiddie matinees for just twenty-five cents. These special events were okay, if you could stand the patronizing "door prizes" (usually pencil boxes and school supplies) and the excruciatingly bad films: *Shinbone Alley; Munster, Go Home!; The Shakiest Gun in the West*. *Shinbone Alley,* a cartoon adaptation of Don Marquis' *Archy & Mehitabel,* remains to this day the only movie I have ever walked out of. But it was a "quality" children's movie shown at the Yorktown, Disney's *Song of the South,* that made me realize I had grown too political for childhood fare.

There is a scene in *Song of the South* where the young white plantation youth, a boy of eight or so, is ordered by his mother to put on his dress clothes—cumbersome, Little Lord Fauntleroy velvet and lace, in the style of the nineteenth century. The boy approaches the hated foppery with a screwed-up and miserable face, his entire body rigid with resistance to enforced feminization. At this moment, every little boy seated near me in the Yorktown Theater yelled out "The poor kid!" or a similar remark of great sympathy. Nothing could be worse than dressing like a girl.

That more sympathy was mustered for the privileged white kid than for the black slave children just offscreen, and that we

as a youth audience in the just-integrated South were manipulated into this racist reaction, made me feel much older, for I
observed that I was quite alone in my specific response to the
screenplay. What was wrong with me? I couldn't even enjoy
kid's movies any more: because I had read *To Kill a Mockingbird* and *The Best Short Stories by Negro Writers* over and over.
Perhaps, I decided then, adult movies would offer more honest politics. I would bike farther afield.

This sent me over to the Center I and II at Lakewood Shopping Center, which was another story altogether. I was free to
enter the glare of GP drama, and every single movie that played
there in the early seventies was disturbing as hell. The Center's
repertoire vacillated between "heavy" movies and exploitation
schlock, the marquee screaming out *Ben. Frogs. Bless the Beasts
and Children. Planet of the Apes. The Exorcist. The Other.* Even
the coming attractions were over my head: *Zardoz, Electra Glide
in Blue, Once Is Not Enough.* But I sat through it all because I
knew that the more GP pictures I saw, the cooler I was in my age
group. And maybe, at some point, there would be a movie with
a twelve-year-old girl in it that would explode the illusion that
one was either a Disney boy or an R-rated adult in America.

The film I remember pinning my hopes on, in my first solo
expedition to the Center I and II, was Jack Lemmon as James
Thurber in *The War between Men and Women.* I had read one
of Thurber's stories; I enjoyed the television program *My
World and Welcome to It,* which featured William Windom as
Thurber and Lisa Gerritsen as the eleven-year-old daughter
who peppered her intellectual father with questions. This television series seemed so like my relationship with my own
father that he and I had watched it together, celebrating young
Lisa Gerritsen's guts in wearing braces with her nightbrace
attached while on television. When the series was made into a
movie I had permission to go see it at the Center I and II. I
went twice.

But it was Thurber's misogyny, the failure of his realtionships with women, which figured largely in the screen version. Lisa Gerritsen, for reasons that were never explained, was no longer portraying a spunky smart girl but a pathological stutterer, whom Thurber "shocks" into a cure by shouting cruel abuse. Thurber himself goes blind during the course of the film, a distressing enough aspect of the talented writer's real life, but compounded infinitely by the woman-hating line at the end: "Blindness does have its benefits, madam. After all, I can't see you."

What was I to make of this? I looped home shakily on my bicycle, knowing I had just been privy to something altogether awkward. Did adult men hate girls and women? Why was the one eleven-year-old girl cast on-screen given a speech impediment, further limiting the efficacy of her power as a speaker? I frowned and snarled and fussed. My father pointed out that Thurber's hostility really came from fear of women, and indicated the well-known cartoon where Thurber draws his house as a giant wife about to swallow him. Not comforted by this interpretation, I gloomily confronted my oncoming puberty years, when I would seemingly be compelled to choose between *Song of the South* or the sexual hostility of adult men whenever I went to the movies.

Solace came at last in the form of *Paper Moon*, which starred a smart little girl—Tatum O'Neal—playing, oh thank you, a smart little girl, one whom no adult could outwit or manipulate. Throughout 1973 I saw this movie over and over, following its rounds as it bounced from one Durham movie house to the next. I took every friend I had to see this movie. This was it, the ultimate in realism: black and white! The Depression! A girl-child who talked back to adults, who lived by her intelligence in tough times without being Shirley Temple! From *Paper Moon* I learned that I, too, could be a successful con artist, since few adults expected cunning in prepubescent girls.

Weekend after weekend I spent my allowance on *Paper Moon*. My mother learned to expect my routine yell, "I'm going to go see *Paper Moon* now, see ya at dinner," as other mothers greeted their children's announcements that they were off to the beloved fishing hole or sandlot ball game.

Knees up, in the dark, there were no rules. I could eat junk food—my mother's prohibition didn't apply to anything ingested in front of a moving picture. There were Chocolate Stars, Goobers, Raisinettes, Powerhouse Bars, Sugar Babies, and Sno Caps out front at the counter, but I was a creature of habit and every time chose the same thing, Jordan Almonds and an orange drink with ice. I crunched my way through the darkness, joyful, irreverent, focused at last.

By the time *Paper Moon* moved to the Northgate Plaza I had seen it so many times I was tempted to let it go. Northgate Shopping Center was the longest bike ride I was permitted to attempt. One paid an athletic price to see a matinee up there; it was even farther than Eagle Stamp and Coin. Nonetheless, I set off one Saturday with dollar in hand and eagerly approached the box office. I was by then just past twelve years old, and happily ripping off the movie theaters of Durham by getting in for the cheaper under-twelve price. But when I asked for "one child, please," the manager at the Northgate refused to sell me a ticket. I hung my head and prepared myself to explain that, all right, I was twelve, but my moral dilemma abruptly switched tracks when he told me to my face that in his opinion, children under seventeen should not see this movie without a parent's signed permission.

I was livid. I knew my rights: anyone could see a GP film. I had already seen this one seven times! Only R-rated movies legally required that persons under seventeen be accompanied by a parent or guardian. I had the money. But it was his call, he was the manager, old daddy law; and he had decided anyone under seventeen who wanted to see a GP film had to bring their parents to the box office to sign a permission slip.

I had to go to a pay phone and phone my father.

"Big Weeg, the manager at the Northgate won't sell me a ticket for *Paper Moon.*"

My father snorted. "Did you try to get in for under twelve again?"

"It's not that. You remember him, he's that square dude with the personal policy about letting kids see good movies. Can you come over on the motorcycle?"

My father had already wrangled with this certain theater manager: the man had tried to prevent my parents from taking me to see Liv Ullman in *The Emigrants,* because he believed it was not suitable for children. (To be fair, if I remember correctly, in that film one character says of another, "She is not happy unless she has a prick inside her as far as it will go.") My father came over on his Kawasaki and exchanged more words with the manager. Months later I had my very first date with a boy at that theater; he ended up setting fire to a popcorn box to impress me, and we were thrown out of the Northgate Plaza on legitimate grounds of delinquent behavior.

4

By the fall of 1973 I had been twelve for half a year, was growing, changing, and everything was coming off or out of me. The orthodontist removed my braces one glorious day. My first period arrived the following week; now I had beautiful teeth, but didn't feel like smiling, as I confronted the decades ahead of strange cramps, wrecked underwear, and expensive "sanitary" products I'd be buying from now on.

To distract me from new womanhood blues, my mother took me to see *American Graffiti,* at the Carolina Theater downtown. That movie, to her, summed up every image of her own adolescence in southern California; and oddly, it became my adolescence too, but as a vicarious rite of moviegoing. It became the gift my mother handed me at puberty, as some mothers pass on pearl necklaces or rings.

For the entire rest of the year I was twelve, I lived and breathed *American Graffiti,* seeing it seven or eight times, each time with my new best friend Jennifer, who was a goddess and popular. We were so entranced by the fifties dance music introduced through the soundtrack that we bought the movie album and played it to one another over the phone every night. This was another routine my mother grew accustomed to: that after dinner I would blast Del Shannon's "Runaway" on our wobbly turntable, and phone Jennifer to make her swoon.

Amused by our obsession with the fifties, my mother taught us how to do the New Yorker, and soon Jennifer and I were bringing the *American Graffiti* album to school every day and dancing to it in the middle school lounge during lunch. We knew every line of dialogue, every song lyric, every nuance of the screenplay. I was spending most of my allowance on *American Graffiti,* and something else was happening: I was being dragged, kicking and screaming, into the teenage world.

There comes a time when every eggheaded bookworm scabby-kneed twelve-year-old girl becomes best friends with someone like Jennifer, someone just that wink of a bit much older, who has graduated from spending her allowance on toys to spending it on boys, and this is a wonderful, terrible thing. In my crushed old hat and my father's white undershirt and my cheap sneakers from Sears, I was still searching for echoes of my life in the movies, but Jennifer had become an actual star right in the Middle School, holding court with male and female admirers daily. Her emotional outbursts thrilled us all; her unique curly handwriting, which none of us dared copy (though at least five of us adopted her g and e), further exalted her poems and stories. We became friends the very day my first period began, because I knew she had had hers and understood about these things. When I told her, she hit me affectionately in the head with a snowball, and called me "cowgirl"—because I was riding the rag, she said.

After school Jennifer would come to my house and play jacks, yelling obscenities when she missed. Then we would go see *American Graffiti* at the Carolina and come home starry-eyed: she over the film's male stars, me over having this incredible girl-woman as my best friend. We never saw any other movie together—there was only that one, and the carpet down to the fourth row at the theater, and the record we played over and over. As long as we sat side by side at the movies, we were no different: her greater popularity, sophistication, and style subsumed by the task before us, of looking up together at the screen which towered over us both. But I drank thirstily from both sources of light: the light from the screen, and the light in Jennifer's eyes.

In all my biking through town, and all the quarters of my allowance, and all my matinee afternoons in the theaters of Durham, I never found a movie about two girls who loved each other. It was not until many years later that I realized I had really spent my allowance searching for that one thing.

My Father's Tears

My dad and I had a fine arrangement. I always thought that he was God, and he, in turn, made me feel certain that I was a genius. With our mutually enormous egos undulating like warm pudding, we boasted and punned our separate ways through life. My dad taught me that power is not the goal: experience is. Time and again he chose not to accept work that would require him to boss others around. When he himself was bossed around he did not take out his frustration by becoming a petty power monger at home; instead, he played volleyball.

Early on I suspected that my dad was not only God but also James Bond, the Professor on *Gilligan's Island,* Tolkein's Gandalf, and James Dean. My dad was not only knowledgeable but hip, cool—able to function naturally in a wide range of scenarios. He strode about comfortably with athletes, mountain hikers, surfers, Buddhists, engineers, musicians, peace activists, beatniks, astronomers, gardeners, and motorcycle enthusiasts. This was the fine art of being on the inside looking in—as opposed to using one's intelligence to be a purely academic and detached observer passing cynical judgment on the myriad subcultures around us.

My dad became this true method actor after he quit acting school, spending his adolescence as the egghead in his guy gang, as the political troublemaker in his academic classes, as one of a handful of Gentiles at a mostly Jewish high school. To be one thing was not only dull but impractical. To know the essence of all roles meant one never had to seem sheerly tourist, bumbling into adventure with patronizing apologies and conspicuous camera gear. Life on earth is the drama. Be the role thrust at you unexpectedly.

My problem was that I was just like my dad, but born a girl-child. I fully expected to be free to investigate those different paths on planet Earth. I expected to travel unmolested through what later proved to be male-only landscapes. I never thought I would be slowed down by gender, and it was crushing to learn, at puberty, that there were few situations where I could come and go as an inconspicuous participant. Not for me the great Brotherhood of Mankind, sampled by Kerouac and Burroughs and their peers; whether traveling on a bus or walking to the grocery store I was prey for men, who constantly interrupted my exploration of life with propositions, whistles, demands, and, later, sexual touching. I realized that I could never be James Bond: I had to worry about safety, and a different kind of survival—the exhausting protection of my body, my virginity.

Where my gender marked me as prey, my intelligence advertised me as predator—not feminine enough. Knowing, or experiencing, too much of the real world made a woman suspect. A "woman of the world" meant one thing: sexual promiscuity, not diplomatic service, although there were many men who conflated the two. A learned woman, I found, is a smart-ass, a castrating bitch, pushy, too assertive, strident, sexless, cold. And a curious girl, as I was as a preteenager, is incorrigible in the eyes of the law, destined to be wayward, wanton, jailbait.

But as a kid in the last years before my body began attracting unwanted attention, I maintained my apprenticeship to my sorcerer father without awareness of gender lines, and he never once diluted or dumbed down the world he offered me. When I began reading and devouring adult books at age eight or nine, he showed me that it was not enough to be intellectually omnivorous; one had to react emotionally to the material. But the only time I ever saw my father cry was at the movies.

I learned he was capable of crying when I was five and my parents took me to see *Born Free*—although I did not see him cry myself and only heard about it later. The summer I was ten, when we moved from Los Angeles to North Carolina, I felt my father's tears, mixed in with my mother's, on a pillow in their unmade bed; they had wept not over the impending move to the East Coast but in response to watching *The Ghost and Mrs. Muir* on television.

But one year after that, I went alone to the movies with my dad for the first time, to see Herman Hesse's *Siddhartha* at the Yorktown Theater in Durham. Seeing *Siddhartha* was a reward I had earned by reading the book first and discussing it with my father.

With typical eleven-year-old impatience, I insisted I understood the text already, and could we please get on the motorcycle and go to the Yorktown before the movie went back to the distributor?

We were almost the only people in attendance. I sat up straight, regally dignified in my claim to understand the movie.

I concentrated so hard that to this day, some twenty-five years later, I can still recall the sweet cadence of the film's sitar music soundtrack. I did not look at my father, because I intended for my posture to make it clear that he had taught me well: I understood this movie, had no need to pester him with questions, like so many children I saw at far simpler movies.

But when, on-screen, Siddhartha's lover died from the bite of a poisonous snake and became lifeless in his arms, and he murmured into her closed face "You have found peace," something made me turn toward my father and there it was, a long tear rolling down his five o'clock shadow. He glanced briefly at me. I didn't say anything. What could this mean? My father never cried. Should I tell my mother? I shrank against the fake velvet.

I knew my father was thinking about two things: the incredible difficulty of the path toward detachment, which stymies most Western dabblers in Buddhism, and his own personal attachment to my mother, who was not at the movies with us because she had recently had surgery on her eyes. I knew we should be at home paying attention to her, not out playing with our brains at this complicated allegorical film where we were the only audience. Now I had seen my father cry because of a movie based on a book: fantasy upon fantasy. Were my father and I people who would rather read about enlightenment than experience it? Did going to a movie with one's father count as family time? as enlightenment time? Where would I file away this image of my father's tears?

I never told anyone about this incident.

One month later, our entire family went to see *Fiddler on the Roof*—the original, three-hour film version with an intermission in the middle; my mother made us all tuna sandwiches to bring in. When we walked out of the theater, we ran into one of the nastier bullies from my summer day camp, lining up to see the next showing with his parents. "Get out your kleenex," my father told this kid and his entire family; "It's a crying movie."

I felt a rush of admiration for my father and looked the bully in the eye. I did not have to say that I had seen my father cry at movies before; it was enough that he made himself vulnerable, like a tomcat luxuriantly rolling on its back, here in a southern parking lot with strangers who might never understand.

The Ram Man

"There's this weird guy who keeps following us around," said my friend Jill, who was, at the time, only ten years old. I was a worldly twelve.

We were standing on the sidewalk of the annual street fair in Chapel Hill on a warm April day. Hundreds of people jammed Franklin Street, which had become a block party enlivened by food stands and craft booths. I estimated that in the casual throng there might be any number of weird guys. We were, after all, in a college party town in the most liberal area of the state, in an era when males still wore long hair and beards.

"No, no, no," explained Jill's best friend Annie, grabbing my arm. "He doesn't *look* weird. He just won't leave us alone. He keeps watching us."

"Okay, show me the dude."

We pushed our way through crowds of happy, beer-scented students. Everything about Franklin Street was familiar turf and comfortable to me, except now there was a new "indoor" complex called NCNB Plaza, which featured a restaurant and a bank and a brand-new theater named The Ram. I had yet to see a movie at The Ram, as I was already a movie snob, preferring theaters that opened flush onto the street with a marquee and a box office you could walk by while you were licking a dripping ice cream cone. I liked a theater you went into for air-conditioning in the summer and then exited, goose-pimpled, directly onto the sweltering pavement. Mall theaters sat awkwardly on my senses.

"He's in *there,*" pointed Jill, indicating the indoor plaza.

"Well, come on," I directed, secretly flattered to be perceived as a caretaker by my young friends.

I was by this time considered a fearless person and a minor hero at school, for two reasons. One, my father had actually taken me on his motorcycle to see an R-rated horror film, *The Exorcist,* which no other middle schoolers were permitted to see. Two, my stoic behavior had impressed everyone a few months before when a mentally ill woman wandered into our school and shouted religious abuse at me. I figured I knew my way around weird people, and was not particularily put off by their behavior.

We entered the cool, dim plaza building, which was ringingly empty because of the street festival. The tile floors breathed coolness up to my hot feet as my old rubber thongs slapped upstairs, toward The Ram.

So this was the new movie house. So pristine it had no scent of popcorn, it was the first freshly constructed cineplex in my world: a place with no past, no history of olden days or war newsreels; the ticket prices posted now had never been lower in a past era, and I, appoaching thirteen, would always be a dozen years older than this place. The movies to be shown here had yet to be made, released, distributed. Everything about this fresh, indoor cinema bellowed of The Future. I shivered.

"That's him," yelled Jill, from behind my elbow.

I caught a glimpse of a sullen face retreating beyond the theater and into an adjacent outdoor patio. I walked briskly toward the patio with Jill and Annie, and upon entering this snack area observed a man in his twenties hunched over a stone bench.

The interesting thing was that he *looked* like a ram. He had curly soft hair, a rounded belly, and kept butting his head forward and pawing the ground and bleating. I wondered if he had cloven hooves.

"He's been bothereing us *all day,*" Annie reminded me.

I marched over to the ram man and demanded of him, "Look, can we help you in some way?" It was the wrong thing to say.

He turned. He carried his erect penis in his hand like a rolled newspaper. His hand moved up and down with blurring speed. At the last minute, he turned to the wall behind the theater and came in wild, sweeping loops against the stone.

Annie and Jill burst into hysterical giggles, astounded at this display of what seemed to be public piss art. I also thought the man was urinating, although why he had chosen to make a Jackson Pollock of it on the new Ram Theater wall was baffling to me. Dazed, I stood there intoning over and over again "Can we help you?"—until he fled and we fled, in different directions.

Down the empty rampway, down the tiled halls, past the new movie house where there was no scent of popcorn, down to the big glass doors and out into the street, where a rush of warm spring dogwood and pizza air enveloped us.

"He did it like this," chortled Jill, mimicking the ram man's technique.

"Gross me out," was Annie's comment.

They were completely relaxed and seemed entertained by it all, whereas I was a nervous wreck. I quickly found Jill's older brother and told him not to lose sight of the girls. Then I went home to my parents and attempted to explain what had happened.

"You have to make a police report," my mother advised. "There's a serial rapist stalking young women at UNC."

The full meaning of what had just happened sank in and I just sat down on the kitchen chair and drank some juice. My father explained that what came spraying out in spiral patterns on the back wall of The Ram was not, in fact, urine, but another substance. Horribly embarrassed, I spent several hours refusing to speak with police, but finally agreed to talk when my parents placed the call for me.

"What was he doing, ma'am? Can you describe exactly?" pressed a soft-voiced Southern police officer. I picked reluctantly at the cork bulletin board by our kitchen phone and mumbled, "Well, he was, like, pulling on himself and he peed all over the wall."

"Can you describe it?" asked the officer.

"Masturbating," I sighed.

"He exposed himself to a group of young girls," my mother chipped in.

"What exactly was he doing, ma'am?" asked the officer.

"He had his penis in his hand and then *stuff* went all over the wall," I shouted, giving the phone back to my parents.

The next day at school I was a folk hero again. Several boys my age came over and started to say smart things, then didn't. All of a sudden I was treated as though I was sexually mature: I had seen an adult male's private parts. My best friend sidled up and informed me "It wasn't piss on the wall, you know," and I knew I would never, ever, sit through a movie at the new Ram Theater—and though I loved movies, I never did.

Reel 2

adolescence

The K.B. Baronet

Few traumas are quite so insulting to the human spirit as transferring from a great alternative school, where "different" kids are secure and well-loved, to a public junior high, where "different" kids are alone and miserable and made fun of. But there I was, at thirteen, wrenched from the warm bosom of Carolina Friends School, and plopped back down on the prickly backside of Western Junior High in Bethesda, Maryland. Even my life as a movie buff could not save me now, I thought, as I rode bus 843 to that first day of school: every movie I had seen on the subject of "the new kid" arriving at a public school ended in horror. *Rebel Without a Cause*, for instance.

These were the mid-seventies in DC's affluent suburbs, after the flower children but just before preppies: the Disco Generation of gauze shirts under polyester, Frye boots under painters' pants, marijuana without love or inspiration, pet rocks, and mood rings. These were my new classmates, looking at me contemptuously from behind reflector shades and curling-iron haircuts. With my tomboy overalls and earnest portfolio of creative writing, I was as alien as a toadstool spore to the wealthy burnout society I'd parachuted into; a countrified queer, a tacky-garbed nobody, a girl who had not had a salon haircut since age six.

Hierarchies popped up faster than I could learn them at Western. The public school system used "tracking" as a matter of policy: each student was diagnosed as smart, average, or stupid, then plugged into classes with other kids from the same category, with not a snowball's chance in hell of transferring to a more appropriate level. It was as blatant as crap on a diaper, and every kid knew exactly where she or he had been pinned on the IQ board as soon as they walked into their first class of the year. Socially, Western was just as hierarchical: there were high-achieving "smart" kids in student government and sports, and, mingled in the "average" and "stupid" classes, the burned-out potheads who flaunted sexuality in the halls and came to school stoned every day. Finally, there were the nerds, academically troubled late bloomers who had not quite caught on to experimentation with sex, drugs, and rock 'n roll.

I gave the guidance counselors a real run for their money, as I came to Western from a notorious alternative school that did not grade students' course work. My transfer files contained no letter grades, only large IQ scores; but how could anyone know if I was a productive good girl or a dangerous con artist?

I became the administration's guinea pig, tried out here and there, tracked into smart-kid English, pothead math, stupid science, and rock bottom juvenile delinquent geography (despite the fact that I could identify more countries than the instructor). There was no consistency in my day, or, indeed, in the expectations of my new teachers. My very classes defined me as normal first thing in the morning, a moron before lunch, brilliant after lunch (when I was too full and sleepy to contribute much), and a moron again at the end of the day.

Every fifty minutes, I changed social and intellectual status, like a Jekyll-and-Hyde entity. It was exhausting.

As a result of the administration's mixed assessment of my brain, few of the students were sure how to stereotype me themselves. The smart kids, embarrassed by my hippie clothing, assumed I was a pothead. The potheads were fairly certain I was a nerd. And the nerds thought I was a smart kid. This revolving door might have served me well, but it was the pothead group, with its cruel clique of sexy party girls, which ruled the halls, and was the least forgiving of difference.

Every day I hurried from stupid science to delinquent geography with a burning face as the ruling groovy girls called me names, tore off my bandanna, stole small objects from my person, and pointed out my presence with "There's that weirdo!" "Look, dress like a girl and they'll like you more," whispered one concerned classmate, who was later kidnapped by a cult and brainwashed. But I wouldn't sell out. It became a peculiar rite of passage, enduring the cruelty of those girls.

Gym was certainly the worst hour of the day. Here, all the different categories of girls were thrown in together, costumed inelegantly in one-piece, zip-front, green-and-white-striped flammable gym suits. Because for this one period athletic prowess, rather than IQ or popularity, determined who was team captain and who was chosen first for daily teams. Smart, average, and stupid girls ended up mingled, free to inflict injury not only on members of the opposing team but on one another as well. The smart girls, competitive in all arenas, since their parents expected good grades in PE as well as academia, seemed to enjoy being pitted against one another and had a high rate of violent injuries. However, a popular pothead on team A would never score against her own gang members on team B, and thus all our sports matches were effectively sabotaged by peer loyalty, while our valiant gym teacher Jackie Thompson sat in the bleachers shaking her head in disgust, wondering why she had campaigned for Title IX.

We bounced balls off each other's bodies in deadly lineups, inept, apathetic. "Is this right?"

"God, you look retarded."

"Was that a point for our team or for theirs?"

"Hell if I care."

"Fuck you."

"Fuck her."

"Eat shit!"

"Lez."

"Homo!"

"Queer!"

"Queer!"

"Lez!"

Because I had been tracked into stupid science and likely-to-fail algebra, to say nothing of reform-school geography, I spent most of my day in classrooms where my abilities were assumed to be negligible, and my peers similarly languished in preordained failure. Naturally, because we were tracked as losers, our course work in the sciences was insultingly pale and weak, further turning us off the subject. The overall result was predictable: I did not do well in math or science and, horribly, began to shrug off my middling grades as acceptable for a girl.

Only in a misogynistic society is ineptitude rewarded; only in a nation pompously confident about masculine technology and resources are young women indulged when they whine "I just don't GET math." Like millions of other young American women, I stopped trying to be the best in my class during junior high. And because I did not demonstrate any precocious capacity in loser math and loser science, the school administration felt justified, even smugly self-congratulatory, for having tracked me into low-level, loser work. The full, vicious circle.

I hated Bethesda, I hated the new school, I hated the students. I was sullen, hostile, uncooperative, sarcastic, judgmental, and alone—using every fiber of my being to wallow in nostalgia for my previous school. I regarded all my new teachers unforgivingly, as pathetic pawns in a corrupt and fascistic system. I grew inward like a toenail until I succeeded in irritating even myself.

Just when I would think to myself "This is it—I'm losing my mind," my parents would rescue me by taking me to the movies. The movies, in Washington, were far more affordable than the private alternative schools.

The theater nearest us was the K.B. Baronet, which was inside a corner building and had a real merry-go-round in the lobby. At very popular first-run movies, parents could stand in line while their children rode the carousel or bought ice cream in the mall. I felt too old for rides, too cynical even for ice cream, so my father distracted me with logic puzzles while we waited in line. He knew I was still good at math and science.

We were stalled in a long and winding line for a new comedy and impatient suburbanites were pressing against one another's backs, as though it would speed up the process.

My father turned to me and said "Now, why can't each person just take one giant step forward, all at the same time?"

I thought about this. "Because there isn't the necessary space to step into, except for the first person in line at the very front. She's the only one who can move forward, once they start letting people in."

"So," my father prodded, "What if that first person took a step?"

"Well, when she moves, she'll free up a stepping space for the person who's second in line. Then person number two can take a step. And that opens up space for person number three. But there's like a delay, okay, for each person in line to take that giant step. So for the entire line to move forward one foot takes . . . "

"How much time?" asked my father.

"The amount of time it takes to step into a foot of space times the number of people in the line plus factoring in the delay between each person," I yawned. "Is that why this is taking so Goddamned long?"

"Is there a different solution?" my father asked me.

"Of course there is; you can blow a whistle, and at the sound of the whistle we could all leap up in the air and over one foot. Then the whole line would have shifted, but you have to calculate that everyone's capable of making that leap, and that the first person in line moves ahead far enough to lead the whole unit over. Not everyone in this line could leap up and over equally. See, there are bunches of little kids; and three people in wheelchairs; and women in dumb pointy high-heeled shoes; and any number of grown-ups like you with back trouble from too much volleyball."

"So what's your conclusion?"

"The most efficient way to move the line forward is not to push and shove, or to leap up and over, but to wait for the open space?" I offered.

"And why won't that solution work, even if you prove it mathematically?"

"Because of the psychological factor."

"And that is . . . ?" my father prompted.

"As soon as any impatient dude in the line sees motion up front at the box office, he thinks it means the whole line is free to push along, so he pushes. Even if there isn't a space to step into yet for him, he feels, like, obligated or something to do at least a small motion forward, to clue the folks behind him that yeah, the line is moving. To spread optimism, I guess. To expand his personal relief into a sort of group experience. To give the sense of progress." I grinned. "We feel obligated as humans to share the sense of progress."

"Move up, buddy," someone told my father, seeing that there was a three-inch space ahead of my father's toes that he had not taken advantage of yet.

"There you go," I concluded.

We were shuffling closer to the box office now. My father, who hated waiting in lines, began wearing what my mother liked to call his "moth face."

I decided to distract him in turn. "Okay, you're at a party, a party chock-full of really cool people you dig and admire, and likewise want to impress. You go into the kitchen for some dip, and while you're there you overhear a bunch of the hottest party guests talking about you. They're about to pay you the ultimate compliment. And that compliment is . . . choose the fantasy that's best for you—that they think you are really SMART, really NICE, or really GOOD-LOOKING. Okay, you can only pick one."

My mother wanted to play this one. "Either nice or good-looking," she decided.

"Either good-looking or smart," my father said.

They both looked at me. "Smart," I said unhesitatingly.

We were finally in the theater. I felt relaxed and smug, seated between my parents, eating popcorn, talking about all the little family in-jokes that one talks about in that wonderful and timeless blank space before the coming attractions begin.

Suddenly, my peripheral vision caught sight of something that sent the popcorn in my belly on a hideous spin cycle. Not four rows over were the meanest, most powerful popular girls from Western Junior High. They were here at my movie en masse. And they had brought their boyfriends.

41

"Jesus!" I choked, sending my mother's cup of iced Fresca flying into the face of an adjacent film critic.

"What on earth is wrong?" my mother gasped, mopping up the mess and examining me with alarm.

"It's them," I hissed in hushed tones, hoping I had not been spotted by yonder coterie of enemies. I peeped out from behind my father's motorcycle jacket until I was sure that they had not seen me. I was reasonably safe—baby bird cuddled between mama and papa bird. But what did it mean, that the girls who were so harsh to me at school liked the same movies as my own impossibly cool parents? What did it mean, that they actually went to the movies, laughed and responded to cinematic stimuli, ate Jordan Almonds in the dark? Were they human, after all? Real? Even—perhaps—like me?

I have no idea, to this day, what the movie was that night, since I spent the entire picture surreptitiously observing my enemies' reactions to it. They laughed when others laughed; they gasped when others gasped; the blue light shining from the screen onto their open, absorbed faces made them seem younger, benign, as innocent and upturned as faces in a July Fourth crowd looking up at fireworks.

They were at this movie without their parents on a school night. Were they dropped off? Did older siblings with drivers' licenses bring them? Did they walk? I had not considered this aspect of their lives, that they too were dependent on grown-ups, or—more likely—were so estranged from their parents that family outings, by this age, were unthinkable. Either way, the humanization of my enemies had begun, in my mind.

My own parents were fond of homilies and moral admonitions, such as "Study your enemies closely, for they are the ones you will most come to resemble," and "Small minds discuss people; average minds discuss events; great minds discuss ideas." I knew that carrying around a heart filled with hatred for these garden variety cruel girls was not best for me in the long run; I would have to outsmart them to survive at school; but part of outsmarting them was understanding them, damn it. I had spoken so easily, waiting in line that night with my father, of how human psychology complicates the easier math of moving people forward. In our junior high, where we were "tracked" into very slow-moving movie lines, into looking up or down at one another, the only categories and subsets we could grasp were rank and pecking order: vertical hierarchies of order, not horizontal unification as students together—or girls. That night I vowed that from then on in school I would find a way to be cool with those girls; and maybe I would even bring up my grades in science.

In the car on the way home my father yawned and frowned. "Well, that was certainly a movie that began well and grew steadily worse," he complained.

"I got a lot out of it," I said.

Function in Disaster

When I was in junior high I knew that at any moment I might be eaten while underwater, consumed in flames, buried alive, crushed by collapsing foundations, washed away in a flood. These same phobias were forced on an entire public through the popular "disaster" films of the mid-seventies, beginning with *The Poseidon Adventure* and continuing through *Earthquake*, *The Towering Inferno*, and, finally, *Jaws*. In these screenplays, natural forces—tides, open-mouthed sea creatures, fire, Mother Earth—claimed lives and bankrupted towns, forcing brave men to face baffling and unpredictable foes. Nothing could have been a more apt symbolism for the impact of the women's liberation movement, which in the exact same period of the seventies was rumbling ominously through the foundations of patriarchal institutions—religion, academia, government. Indeed, as a fourteen-year-old whose parents subscribed to *Psychology Today*, I was well aware of the debate over whether *Jaws* particularly frightened the male population because of the shark's symbol as vagina dentata.

However, because disaster films were deliberately packaged to show a minimum of sex and a maximum of gore, sexual and political symbolism were not high on the list of audience's expectations. Parents felt comfortable sending adolescents to these movies, as any thought-provoking or romantically arousing sequences were vastly outweighed by action footage of uniformed, male authority figures saving lives. Consequently, young people in huge numbers—the eight-to-eighteen market—had parental permission to sit in the dark and watch death and loss and fear and dismemberment drip on-screen, with a background of weeping survivors searching for dead sweethearts amid the rubble. My generation was thus well-trained to view the Oklahoma City bombing and the devastation of Yugoslavia with the numbness of adolescent moviegoers.

My brother and I saw *The Poseidon Adventure* three times, and laughed anxiously throughout it. We argued over whether the hit song "The Morning After" was religious and, therefore, inappropriate for Casey Kasem's Top Forty, which was already playing a nun's controversial rendition of the Lord's Prayer. I later read *The Poseidon Adventure* book, which contained far more scenes of hostility between the female characters than I'd expected.

Earthquake and *The Towering Inferno*, commonly referred to as "shake and bake" at my junior high, generated much more introspection. I was never a squeamish kid, and of course I had trained myself not to have nightmares. However, I certainly believed in being prepared and organized in the face of disaster, and these two films forced me to confront the pressing question of how to preserve my written work.

My parents actually took us to see *The Towering Inferno*, at some suburban shopping center like the K.B. Congressional Plaza—a violation of their every movie rule. Family outings to increasingly expensive first-run movies were rare: we almost always went to the dollar double features at the Circle Theater on Pennsylvania Avenue, a repertory institution beloved by Washington literati. Any first-run movies my parents risked investing in had to leave them with an "up" feeling, or feature classical music, or be romantic and artistically moving. For years it seemed that the only movie we saw as a family was *Fantasia*, over and over. But there we were at *The Towering Inferno*, probably as a special treat for my brother's eleventh birthday.

I spent the entire movie mentally rearranging my room. If I smelled smoke one night while asleep in bed, and had to leap out the window while coughing and gagging, would I have the foresight and/or presence of mind to gather my dearest possessions? What, in fact, were my dearest possessions? My girl-gang friends and I were constantly writing wills and leaving our clothes to each other, but without a doubt my most valued artifacts were flammable paper products: my journals. My scrapbooks. My folders of creative writing. In short, the archives of a self.

Very well, then; if I insisted upon keeping these vulnerable items in my house, I should obviously keep them all in one neatly trussed bundle right by my bedroom door! Then, in an emergency (such as fire), I could grab the bag and escape with the memorabilia intact. The instant we arrived home from the movie (with my mother whispering "poor Jennifer Jones" over and over), I resolutely reordered my favorite things, going so far as to measure them for a canvas knapsack. At the sight of the knapsack itself, however, I stopped cold. I realized in that moment that I was the same age as Anne Frank, who had, under far less imaginative circumstances, also made a fast inventory of whether her journal could fit into an escape satchel.

No Jew living after the events of the Nazi Holocaust has not, at some point, envisioned the scenario of The Knock on the Door and deportation. We ask ourselves what we would have done—resist? go quietly?—and we tell ourselves it could happen again, or that it must never happen again. This inner process begins in childhood. Anne Frank's diary, the documentary film reels of Belsen (where she perished) narrated by Trevor Howard, and the testament of survivors and their liberators were real disaster screenplays I had internalized forever as a teenage Jew.

Much later, as a professor of history, I would debate those tired and bitter questions of whether Europe's Jews could have seen the Holocaust coming, should have fled early on, should have fought back at every juncture. But even at fourteen I could grasp that for most of us there is no preparation for the unspeakable. To be the first person prepared for a consequence others believe impossible is to earn oneself a reputation for paranoia. Like Anne Frank, I had lived a protected, educated, middle-class life. Would fireproofing my suburban bedroom train me, in any way, for surviving, say, ethnic violence?

What does one pack to begin an identity as a survivor?

I sat through much of high school absorbed by this question.

Finally, some years later, I wrote a poem based on that moment of seeing myself as a Jewish girl in flight.

Someone is coming soon, so I work
furtively, feverishly, packing what I
see. What

I remember, will need to eat, feel, see
in transit, in hiding, in extremis.
Paper, ink. A fountain pen

is handy, is hollow, is conducive
to smuggling, forging, marking.
Paper, ink,

a comb. Weighs nothing, creates dignity
in filth, in stink, disorder. A camera
would be stupid, naming me

a spy. We archivists are first to die,
bad busybodies, throwbacks, liars
so, no letters, books, or film.

Create escape: don't witness now,
don't waste air watching; all fall
down. Paper. Ink. Comb. A jacket

deep with many linings. Pictures
old enough to bear no tales
of resistance, at-risk lovers.

Just to look at, not to use. A
knife, a toothbrush, stuff for bribes,
flat flask of liquor, hard bread, socks.

This isn't summer's camping trip.
The doorbell is a hangman's knot
if someone rings it now, for me

before I'm down the toilet-pipe
over the fence
through sewage drains, and

faster than the smoke they make
of my tribe's bodies
I'll be out.

The will to survive could carry me out of a window, or across
borders, as necessary; and realistically I felt protected from Jew-
burning in my liberal community. But what about nuclear war?
This loomed over us all. What could a nuclear war survivor's

knapsack possibly contain to prolong life? Bottled water, I thought; gauze, liquor (for trade). My father told me to forget it; that in global nuclear war the dead were the fortunate ones, that the survivors were doomed to a slower and worse extinction.

For a while I had two packed knapsacks in my room. One for a house fire, packed with personal treasures; one for a planetary fire, packed with medicine. Then, just when I thought I was really well-prepared, I saw *Earthquake*.

Forget "Sensurround": like most Californians, I've lived through several earthquake disasters, and there is simply no authentic imitation of that thunder-rumble beneath your bed. I grew up knowing what to do in an earthquake and listening for the warning cries of dogs. My father's attitude was even more blasé; he went right back to sleep after the spring 1970 earthquake (which literally threw L.A. out of bed). As California natives, my brother and I were frequently asked to describe our earthquake experiences for show-and-tell amusement when we transferred to East Coast schools. We went to see *Earthquake* for the sheer privilege of commenting knowledgeably, amid East Coast audiences, about aftershocks and Richter scales and "The Valley." Then, while reading news articles about disaster rescue workers, I discovered a writer's worst disaster scenario.

After earthquakes or tornadoes, many survivors returned to find that their houses, while still standing, were roped off by authorities and judged "unstable"—meaning the buildings had to come down. The former owners, I read on with increasing rage, were seldom allowed to go back inside to retrieve any of their belongings—treasured photo albums, children's toys, or— the clincher—unpublished manuscripts. (This was well before the era of floppy disks and computer backup files.) The hapless disaster victims would plead and weep, to no avail. They were simply not permitted to re-enter the condemned structure, which, in defense of rescue authorities' strict mandates, really could collapse in a twink during the merest aftershock.

Knowing that there were persons who could tear down my house without letting me get to my journals filled me with panic. I was prepared to defend my writing against any natural or human forces of disaster. My own teen mortality barely mattered: my stories had to survive. I mentally ticked off the roster of authority figures looming between me and my writing. English teachers, who in my loathsome public junior high denounced creative writing as a frill. Nazis, who burned books and Jewish girls simultaneously, with pyromaniacal indifference. And now firemen! Emergency crewmen! Building inspectors! Disguised as benevolent rescuers, these uniformed bogeymen could prevent me from reaching through a perfectly accessible bedroom window to grab my sheaf of manuscripts.

I spent hours rehearsing the dreaded confrontation. "I'm sorry, little lady; we can't let you in there. I know it looks safe, but believe me, any moment that wall can crumble. You'll just have to write new stories."

"No! NO-O!" I race past the fireman. He catches me by the back of my overalls and wrestles me to the ground. Overhead, the court-ordered wrecking ball dangles like a malevolent horse turd, poised to smash my journals into pulp.

"Backup! I need backup RIGHT NOW!" shouts the fireman—but I kick and punch my way from his grasp and race across the DO NOT CROSS rope lines to my broken bedroom window. I am inside with the agility of a cat and in one swift motion scoop my writing into my arms. A small chunk of plaster disengages from the ceiling, grazing my braids, but I emerge unharmed. Triumphant. I win. HA!

The fireman is furious. So is the police chief, the mayor, the county clerk, the engineer crew, the President of the United States—somehow they are all there in our front yard, wagging their big fingers, shaming me. I am going to jail. My parents are made to pay an enormous fine. The rest of our house is quickly demolished.

In reform school they take away my fountain pen, claiming it could be used as a weapon, and force me into an ugly plaid uniform. As I slip into my new clothes, my new roommates (all blonde and burly, with forbidden cigarettes dangling between chapped lips) ask what I did to get sent to Juvi. I say, "I broke into my own house," and hug my journals fiercely to my breasts.

I tortured myself with these fantasies. I studied the legal ramifications. Could I sign a document absolving the city of any responsibility, put on a hard hat, and have four minutes to go back into the house? By whose authority could some GUY say no? Was there a board of engineers one could petition, with a special jury for writers whose homes had been damaged in an earthquake?

My mother finally suggested that if I was so concerned about fires and earthquakes damaging my journals I should buy a large, steel box and keep my writing in a bank vault. I munched on this for a while, but I really wasn't ready to be quite that prepared. Perhaps I'd been taking myself too seriously. Perhaps I'd been seeing too many disaster movies.

Eventually, the school year ended and I found myself at the beach with my girl-gang—every last one of whom seemed obsessed with the new movie *Jaws*.

I had already read Benchley's book. I refused to see the movie for ten years afterward, because of the chapter in the book where the young marine biologist asks Ellen Brody to describe her sexual fantasies and she immediately answers "Rape, I guess." That a police chief's wife would casually remark (as a bid for seduction, yet!) that most women's ordinary fantasies began with violent sexual assault made my stomach hurt. This chapter, of course, did not in any way appear in Spielberg's movie. But I knew it was integral, in the book, to the nervous Chief Brody's decision to risk fighting a shark: he had to win back and excite his ambivalent wife.

While my friends squealed at the water's edge and looked for imagined sharks, endlessly debating whether a girl with her period should even approach the tides, I was diving into the surf and riding waves. One afternoon I looked up from the ocean and realized that I was usually further out to sea than any other female at that Eastern Shore beach. No other girl my age was really there to swim. They were all mincing along the boardwalk, trying to meet guys.

I could prepare myself for disaster; protect myself from loss. But there was no way I could protect my friends from what might happen to them in the normal course of summertime dating and sexual intitiation. Every guy who read Benchley's book would read and believe that normal women longed for rape. My friends were far more likely to be attacked by the guys they met than by sharks. And I wondered why no one ever made a disaster movie about that.

The Girl-Gang Movies

It was Lindsey's voice on the phone, so my heart sped up. "We're going to the movies," she commanded, in her bored and regal way. It was the summer of 1975, and we were fourteen, bored and regal as fourteen-year-old girls will be.

"Cool, which movie?"

"Same as usual, duh, at the K.B. Georgetown Square. My mom's driving, we'll pick you up. Don't wear that stupid hat, please."

Lindsey was entitled to speak to me this way because she was the queen bee and I was a drone; I didn't really care. I readied myself for another heavenly afternoon at the only double feature I went to with my girl-gang, that brilliantly paired tribute to forbidden love between eccentric nonconformists, *Harold and Maude* and *The King of Hearts*.

I joined a girl-gang in junior high, a loose but judgmental cluster of prelesbian Christian brainy girls. Although I was a Jew, rather than a member of the Methodist youth group all these girls attended, I decided that this was the right gang for me. I made this decision after I went to a party at Lindsey's house near the end of eighth grade, where we played all-night party games that involved hugging and kissing each other with the greatest of tenderness. Starving for affection, like a cringing young dog, I experienced conversion, confusing the holy kiss of Christianity with the intense same-sex friendships I observed in process before me. I felt I had joined a caravan of protective and generous wise women, all absorbed in dallying with one another on their languid jouney toward that Eastern Star. And the desert led seductively in every direction.

After this my journals sang of desire and love in the present day, not just the past days of my years in Durham; page after page of CRUSH, CRUSH, CRUSH, willingly spiraling from the recording of herstory to my own participation in creating it. I was a teenager folding lesbian possibility into my writing life like an origami dragonfly, a life that would be motion as well as paper, and change of body as well as change of schools.

Initiation into a gang, into a secret culture or a religious sect of any kind, requires a sacrifice on the part of the initiate. In fraternity traditions there is hazing, which brings the hapless pledge symbolically (or actually) close to the portals of death through physical stress. The pledge loses his previous, individual/outsider status in a vacuum of alcohol or reckless play, reemerging as an accepted brother amid brothers.

In the real gangs of the streets, initiation involves more than mere bodily and psychological humiliation, often extending to tattooing, bloodletting, scarring, even the ultimate "manhood" test of killing a member of a rival gang.

But for middle-class women in American society, sorority and girl-gang pledging are more likely to involve acts of obedience to the high priestess leader. One may be forbidden to speak, or forced to speak only in rhyme during Hell Week, forced to signify to the head señorita when she alone commands. The power of language to control persons seeking acceptance is certainly at the center of such traditions. (My aunt Pat, who was accepted into the most prestigious girls' social club in her sophomore year at L.A. High, recalls pledge week as "Sort of a week of being this doggy person. It was, carry my books, pledge; walk four steps behind me, pledge; oops, I spilled my Coke, pledge, why don't you wipe it up with the hem of your poodle skirt?")

I did not expect anything like this as part of my acceptance into the close-knit girl culture of my new friends, but I was wrong. At first I was tolerated at their lunch table, as a curiosity, a sort of personality specimen bottle. When I joined their Methodist youth group in a greater effort to be one of the gang, I won a few nods of approval. Lindsey seemed very fond of me and shepherded me around, throwing her other followers into conflict and jealous rage, but I did not grasp that I had come in as an interloper, distracting the head goddess whom they all loved.

They got even. One night not long after school had let out for summer, all the girls but Lindsey sat me down on a curb beneath a streetlight, and told me I could not be one of them unless I stopped writing in my journal. They said that in this gang there were no secrets, and that I could not be permitted to continue writing down emotional information rather than speaking it to everyone's face.

"You're, like, totally dependent on your journal," said one girl. "It's just serving to, like, divide us," pronounced another. "It's not you," sighed a third; "it's your stupid piece of shit notebook that we can't accept."

Depsite the hum of June cicadas, and the buzzing of the streetlight casting its white circle around us, I could hear them all thinking. And they were thinking: GOTCHA.

The GOTCHA of my initiation was that I had to give up writing if I wanted a place in the gang. They had me, all right; the whole event might have been choreographed. There I sat, all weaknesses and vulnerabilities exposed, forced to choose between writing and popularity, between personal power and an assured place in a community of women. They knew I had no friends, wanted their hugs, would indeed give anything to sit at Lindsey's right hand. The price of such luxury was the ultimate sacrifice. I must give up what was most precious to me: in this case, my writing.

All right, I thought frantically. I could not bear the idea of returning to my solitary existence after sampling the realm of girlfriends. I would die for their sins, become Christ-like, further transcending my Jewishness; I would humble myself, denounce my writing as vanity; if I did this they might hold me in their arms.

I agreed to it all, crouching, whipped, at their Dr. Scholled feet. I said yes, I will stop writing. The words of my initiation pledge fell around me in the wet grass like the locks of hair shorn abrasively from a new military recruit. Behold the tendrils of your old identity, O voyager; we will remove from you everything of your past persona, and rebuild you as one of us, the few, the proud, the secret elite.

Unexpectedly, Lindsey materialized and slipped a necklace of beads over my head. I had noticed that all her other followers wore this. "Now you're one of us," said Lindsey, smiling at me. Yes. Like them, like most American girls, I would give up the best I had to offer the world in exchange for a place at the cafeteria lunch table; I would learn to abandon all intellectual and professional goals in the interest of popularity and acceptance.

We all walked in the dark for hours, then slept in a pile on somebody's waterbed. "Here, give me your hand," said Lindsey, her touch sending waves of what I would later call arousal across my solar plexus. I recognized the strange new feeling I had hitherto only experienced at Lindsey's party that spring. Well and good, then. No one had asked me to give up that sensation, that magnificent swoop, that always unanticipated pinwheel of love. I was not numb after all, not anesthetized by any means. I still had Lindsey's hand in mine when I fell asleep that night, clutching my new necklace of beads; journalless, washed clean.

I spent the entire summer at the movies with this gang, and every outing was the same, *Harold and Maude* and *The King of Hearts*. There were certain advantages to the double feature format: many of our mothers were delighted to have our temperamental hormones out of the house for a chunk of time, and spoke wistfully to one another of their own youth, when going to the movies included not just a double feature but a newsreel and a cartoon and a serial drama, and all for a dime. We in turn relied on the length of the double feature for other reasons: by rotating our seats in between the two films, at least four girls got to sit next to Lindsey.

We all pretended to be on diets, and were careful not to eat anything fun in front of one another, so we brought our own popcorn to the movies, seasoned with Lemon-Pepper and Crazy Mixed Up Salt. The first movie was always *Harold and Maude,* gay Colin Higgins's wonderful story of the morbid young man who falls in love with a spirited seventy-year-old woman. The soundtrack consisted of songs by Cat Stevens; we had all his albums and went to see him in concert. But no one in our gang really identified with either Harold (male) or Maude (old); nor did we find it necessary to declare that we found Harold cute, or even Cat Stevens; the point of attending this movie was to share in the thrill of socially disapproved romance, and the oddly matched lovebirds' defiance. This daring is what made us cry, although of course we said we cried because Maude dies in the end.

The King of Hearts was even better, because it combined a profoundly antiwar sensibility with sympathy for people whom society has judged crazy. Here Alan Bates portrayed a World War I private sent to defend a French village from German explosives; but unbeknownst to him, the "real" villagers have been evacuated and only the inmates of the insane asylum are left behind, posing as confident townsfolk. Who is crazier—the military forces bent on destruction, or the gentle lunatics in their borrowed finery? Alan Bates falls in love with Genevieve Bujold and elects to throw in his lot with her craziness, with her own culture of eccentric peers. The film was a teenage nonconformist's Bible.

And, even better, it was in French!—a boon to our brainy-girl hearts; surely we were the only gang from Western Junior High to attend foreign films, we thought. The double feature satisfied our multiple psychic dietary needs: snobbery, eccentricity, desire, long hours of holding each other's hands with lemon-peppered fingers.

"I am the King of Hearts," one of us would say, in the car going home afterward; the rest of us present would respond on cue, "Sire! Can it be?" Our mothers moaned with weariness at this routine, suggested that we see other movies, or, even better, that we just shut up and get summer jobs.

The triumph of those judged insane moved us deeply because we were surrounded, at school, by spooky authority figures, who could and did expel difficult students or label them disturbed. We all knew girls whose parents had had them committed—because their daughters had been caught having sex, or smoking dope, activities we were interested in ourselves. We knew that our good grades, our ability to play the game of responsible behavior, were all that protected us from being pronounced crazy, because left on our own we did unspeakable things: sucked each other's toes, pretended we were cover models for lesbian magazines, made ourselves vomit.

There was an unspoken agreement that normal behavior was boring and bourgeois, but exactly how far we might skitter into abnormal behavior was a good question. "There's a little bit of lesbianism in us all," assured one girl as she stroked my face in Lindsey's canopy bed; this, I felt, was technically not as dangerous as the abnormal behavior of a kid in our school who set her mother's house afire. But it felt quite as hot and scary.

All through that one summer I was forbidden, by these new friends, to write in my journal. Later I understood their sad hostility toward my writing, for girl after girl at our junior high was "caught" experimenting with drugs or sex when her concerned mom read her diary. Famous men, explorers, could leave diaries and journals of their ventures. Girls burned their diaries at fifteen because our writings served only to convict us—and our friends—of pushing the limits of good-girl behavior.

There could be no record of those times, those games in bed, that movie hand-holding and how it made us feel, and someone like me who saved such times on paper was a threat indeed, to all our freedoms. We couldn't drive, couldn't go out to any jobs but baby-sitting; movies were the only place besides school we might ask to be taken to. Sitting in the dark, free fantasy was possible, our linked hands a seal of girl-gang loyalty.

Steven Spielberg's Cousin

John K. was the original really nice guy. We dated, sort of, in junior high, if dating means many spirited nights at the movies without really getting to "first base." He once paid for my movie, though, with a fifty-dollar bill, which I found very impressive at the time. He scrawled in my yearbook "You'll definitely be a writer," and didn't need to sign it "Love"—the vote of confidence was enough.

Together we saw *Romeo and Juliet* and *Psycho* and a host of Mel Brooks films. John loved movies, and casually asked me if I'd like to be his date at the Academy Awards that year; his cousin was a big director, he said, and his whole family was flying out to Los Angeles. This seemed too fantastic to be true, and anyway I had no money for airfare, so I simply laughed and forgot about the invitation. Months later John explained that his cousin was Steven Spielberg, who had just directed *Jaws*.

I liked John a lot. He showed a good sense of humor toward the anguished murk of teen sexuality. When, at sixteen, I finally wrote in my journal "I think I am a lesbian," I phoned John in a panic. His sensible response was "Why don't we go see this new gay movie, and you can tell me your reactions to it?"

In 1978, if you wanted to see a respectable gay movie, you went to the Circle Theater on Pennsylvania Avenue across from George Washington University. The Circle was a repertory theater that took great pride in selecting appropriately paired films, charging two dollars for a double feature and catering to a loyal clientele of film students, academics, rebels, old hippies, and street people. My parents began taking my brother and I down to the Circle to see classic films soon after we moved to Washington. One of the films we saw was *Steppenwolf,* which had a brief but gripping scene in which one gorgeous woman kissed another on the lips. Another film was *Jonah Who Will Be 25 in the Year 2000*, in which the French actress Miou-Miou tosses off the line that in prison many women become lesbians. But these fleeting glimpses of adult lesbianism were all I ever experienced at the movies, particularly as I was still forced by law to bring a parent to anything rated R.

In contrast, it was fairly easy to see gay male life depicted on-screen, usually in a disparaging way; for years the Circle showed a very popular double bill, *The Boys in the Band* and Michael York in *Something for Everyone*. My mother even took me to see Craig Russell's inspired drag film, *Outrageous!,* at the Circle, because I was interested in acting and she felt I was old enough to appreciate drag performance art as a theatrical genre. But I was so desperate to encounter a positive screen relationship between two attractive and sane women that I was, at home, reduced to watching *Laverne and Shirley*, or television reruns of *Mary Tyler Moore* bantering with Rhoda; later on, it was *Charlie's Angels* and *The Bionic Woman*.

During those first adolescent years when I openly loved women, Hollywood propoganda still insisted that real women hated women. In the movies, women were competitors for the pool of men, catty and jealous enemies sneering through clenched smiles. Even when adult women were portrayed as talented achievers and artists they were bitter rivals, like Shirley MacLaine and Anne Bancroft in *The Turning Point*. A woman might appreciate having her woman friends about her, but only to console her when some man had dumped her, like Jill Clayburgh in *An Unmarried Woman*.

A half century before, Virginia Woolf had written in *A Room of One's Own:*

> . . . how interesting it would have been if the relationship between the two women had been more complicated. All these relationships between women, I thought, rapidly recalling the splendid gallery of fictitious women, are too simple. So much has been left out, unattempted. And I tried to remember any case in the course of my reading where two women are represented as friends.

In my own generation, television and film had hardly improved the situation. It was nearly impossible to find a movie about two women, let alone two women who got along, or, beyond that, actually daydreamed romantically about one another. At sixteen, I was deeply into the phenomenon of daydreaming romantically about women, and dared not talk about this to anyone but John K., who by now had learned to expect just about anything from me.

"Cool," I told him, trembling in my platform sandals and Zen cologne. "I suppose this gay movie's at the Circle?"

"No, it's a real-live, first-run deal at the K.B. Baronet."

"Where we saw *Romeo and Juliet*? Holy shit."

"I know."

Here was a fresh dilemma. Would I be more conspicuous as a young lesbian if I went to a mainstream gay movie in a K.B. theater? At the Circle Theater, all the beatnik regulars blended in together. My family saw virtually every film that came there. When I saw gay movies at the Circle I was simply assumed to be an omnivorous film student, not a teenage gynovore. On the other hand, if I went to the K.B. with John as my escort, everyone would assume we were a voyeuristic straight couple, and somehow this wasn't the impression I wanted to exude either. I walked around the kitchen, twisting the phone cord; later that night it would spring out like a giant coiled snake when my mother tried to order a pizza.

"Fine, John, pick me up tonight—you have your driver's license now, right?"

"What's up with yours?"

"Come on, dude, you try learning to parallel park a Volkswagon bus."

"Okay, I'll get you at seven."

That was how I got to see Meg Foster and Perry King in *Different Story,* probably one of the most disappointing "gay" movies ever made. But it was the first one I saw which featured a lesbian couple. And I saw it with the first straight friend I ever came out to, in the summer of 1978.

Different Story is about a lesbian and a gay man who meet and decide to have a marriage of convenience. In the film this is not a choice based on considerations of respectability, but because the gay man's immigration status is threatened and he needs American citizenship: the old "green card" wedding. In time, however, the lesbian and the gay man fall in love, abandoning their queer communities. The lesbian's neurotic, weepy ex-lover sticks a gun in her face, and the gay man, delighted by his newfound heterosexuality, runs off and fucks another woman just to test-drive his machismo. I sat limply through the parade of ugly stereotypes, hoping in vain for a character I could relate to, admire, or even put up with at all for ten minutes.

"Oy vay," growled John.

"Oh, man," I sighed.

It was the sobbing, suicidal lesbian girlfriend that did me in. Valerie Curtin specialized in such space-case roles, having played the panicky waitress Vera in *Alice Doesn't Live Here Anymore* three years prior to *Different Story*. Seeing her lesbian character on-screen, a closeted teacher who broke down in midconversation, was dependent on her therapist, and grabbed a weapon in response to being dumped, I thought: this is what's in store for me? Either becoming this creature—or dating her?

Even a full box of Jordan Almonds couldn't erase the bitter taste from my mouth this time.

I stomped out to John's car afterward. "Drive," I commanded.

We drove out to the empty parking lot of a private school John had attended as a kid. "Well, that was heavy," he said.

"Look, if I can trust anyone, it's you," I said. "I've spent the entire week reading a book called *Rubyfruit Jungle* and I know I'm in love with my best friend, Carrie. I write her poems and dedicate them to her last name, so if anyone finds my journal they'll think I'm writing about some GUY. I can't believe I'm this chickenshit."

"Wow, so you really think you're gay?"

"I don't want to label myself anything yet," I exploded. "I mean, so what about what I am; it's just HER I'm attracted to. I've liked other girls, too, but the entire implication of homosexuality is frightening to me. It feels like I'm denying my biological function or something. That's what all the Anita Bryant campaigners say. I don't want to end up like that schizo suicidal girlfriend in the movie. Do you think I'm perverted?"

John sighed. "Look, with a guy it's pretty hard to deny when you're turned on by someone and in a state of arousal. The erection is right there. I don't know what it's like for you, to have feelings for another girl. You don't get an erection. How do you feel when you're turned on? You don't have to answer," he added quickly as I turned brick red in the moonlight.

"No, I—I want to talk." I took a deep breath. I thought about my best friend Carrie and a field party we'd attended earlier that summer. We had both been drunk, and her current boyfriend, a preacher's son, drove us home, a fairly long and sultry drive through back roads and honeysuckle air. The two of them cuddled in the front seat while I twisted, dizzy and jealous, in the back. Then Carrie adjusted her seat lever so that she was leaning way, way back, resting with her head more or less between my legs. The wind through the open windows of the Cutlass Supreme sent her hair flowing over my damp forearm. I hovered my hand over her face, not daring to touch her, for half an hour; finally, I rested my fingers on her cheek.

I opened my mouth. "I get these tingly sharp twinges in my stomach that spread to my neck and my toes, and I feel warm all over, and my mouth goes dry, and I . . . smile a lot."

"Hmmmm," said John.

"What does it feel like to have an erection?" I shot back.

He explained.

"What about an orgasm. Do you have them?" I inquired.

"Um . . . yeah," he agreed cautiously. "So . . . you don't?"

"Not when I'm AWAKE, no. But during some of my dreams, YES."

"So what do you want her to do? Anything?"

I thought about this for a long time and finally spoke again. "I guess I want her to be turned on enough to want me. Jesus Christ, I know she'd be a good lover!—she talks all the time about the ways she teases her boyfriend in bed. But oh, John, if I ever talked about any of this to her, she'd just freeze over and dump me as a friend. Her family is pretty conservative, you know? I promised myself that sometime before our high school graduation I'd tell her how I feel. But that gives me another whole year in the closet."

"A frustrating situation," said John.

"She kissed me good night once," I added. "On my birthday."

"I don't think it's wrong, or that you're perverted," John said seriously. "When you talk about her you look radiant and glowing."

I smiled back at him, Steven Spielberg's cousin. "Thank you for seeing the real me, this once. More and more I realize the only way I can grow is up."

"So come out of the closet," he said.

When I came back down from the hill where John and I had this first, hesitant conversation, I was no braver, no closer to telling Carrie that I loved her; but I had a sense that my life, my great well of feeling, was truer than the heinous motion picture we had seen. There simply was no movie for me, yet— a conclusion I seemed to reach annually, at eleven, at twelve, at thirteen or fourteen or fifteen. But there would be a movie, someday soon, I thought, and meanwhile role models for survival might be found in many other places. I finished reading *Rubyfruit Jungle,* for one thing.

Julia: Love between Women as a Slap in the Face

In a 1976 article in *The New York Times,* Jane Fonda said of *Julia,* "It's about a relationship between two women. It's not neurotic or sexually aberrent." Asked by interviewer Judy Klemesrud in an October 1977 *New York Times* issue whether there were overtones of lesbianism in the film, Vanessa Redgrave responded, "No, I don't think so, not at all."

—Raymond Murray, *Images in the Dark*

The most violent defense of the purity of a female friendship on-screen occurrs in *Julia* (1977), when John Glover indelicately suggests that Hellman and Julia have been sexually involved. For this insult Jane Fonda delivers a knockout punch that expresses more anger than she showed at the Nazi threat.

—Vito Russo, *The Celluloid Closet*

Each year I join thousands of other lesbians and head for the famous Michigan Womyn's Music Festival. I have made this pilgrimage every August since 1981, when I was twenty. My friend and festival pal, Toni Armstrong Jr., says that women's music festivals are the answer for all of us who never had sex during adolescent pajama parties. But I think there's another story behind the popularization of the woman-loving camp out. How many of today's festiegoers were, like me, influenced by the film *Julia*, where we saw two adult women pledge love to one another around a campfire's glow?

Because there never was another movie like this. There never was a moment more vulnerable, dramatic, and romantic than that scene where Jane Fonda, as Lillian Hellman, tells Vanessa Redgrave "I love you, Julia," and Vanessa Redgrave, as the heroine Julia, sits proud and tall and wild, holding Jane.

During my last three years as a teenager—1978 to 1981—*Julia* was the only movie in my life, the sanctum sanctorum of my brooding adolescent lesbianism. The film is an adaptation of Lillian Hellman's short story (from *Pentimento*) about her beloved childhood friend, who became an antifascist activist and was subsequently murdered by Nazi agents.

For a short story, *Julia* covers much of the landscape of Hellman's life, but seldom dwells on her groundbreaking play about homophobia—*The Children's Hour*, based on a trial of two schoolteachers accused as lesbians. Instead, *Julia* is an extraordinary tribute to the friend whose convictions often baffled even Hellman. The impassioned Julia moves from their teenage games in America to medical studies with Freud in Vienna, then to radical socialism, and finally uses her family fortune to save Jews and political prisoners in Hitler's Europe. Hellman, at first reluctant and frightened, is enlisted to assist her childhood friend's resistance work by playing courier, and, though a Jew herself, travels by train through Nazi Germany with Julia's money. Soon after their clandestine meeting to exchange the smuggled booty which will save one thousand lives, Julia is brutally murdered, and Hellman begins a fruitless search for Julia's hidden baby—a baby named for Lillian.

"Based on a True Story," shrieked the marquee poster, which I bought from the distributor and tacked onto my closet door at home. Critics argued about whether the film was really a lens for inspecting A) women's friendships, B) socialism and Nazism, C) the life of moody, blacklisted playwright Lillian Hellman. Since only B shifted the focus away from emotive, heroic women to male action and rhetoric, *Julia* became classified as a "women's movie," like *The Turning Point,* which came out in the same period but focused instead on the hateful competition and jealous rivalries between women.

I saw *Julia* for the first time when I was seventeen, with a friend whose father had survived the concentration camps at Bergen-Belsen (where Anne Frank died). It was a period of my life when I was awakening, pop-eyed, to the legacy of the Holocaust which was my own family's history but had hardly been addressed in my schooling at all. I was reading any book I could find on Jewish history and resistance, and of course in those nascent years of the women's history movement in academia there were very few texts which mentioned women's roles in the Jewish community or Nazi resistance. An insightful adult friend, who saw me struggling to locate my identity as a Jew and as a woman writer, recommended seeing *Julia.* Thenceforth I lived on a steady diet of Jane Fonda and Vanessa Redgrave and their campfire embrace, over and over, until I could feel the flames of that campfire and the flames of Nazi Germany licking at the nape of my neck.

Interestingly, the young Julia was portrayed by an actress who had graduated from my very own school in Maryland, Walt Whitman High. The adult Julia was of course portrayed by the unutterably gorgeous Vanessa Redgrave, and I learned that this casting choice had troubled many in the American Jewish community. Redgrave had recently caused havoc by supporting the PLO and denouncing Israeli Jews as "Zionist hoodlums," and yet she'd won several pivotal screen roles as an agent of Jewish resistance (*Julia, Playing for Time*). Some Jews urged a boycott of *Julia*, and I—torn between Judaism and lesbianism—found I could not forego the power of the movie and its actresses, even while I was pining over an Israeli girl at my high school.

Like many young feminists I had been starving for a movie storyline about women's political convictions and losses and intense love for one another, with male characters in the definite background scenery, and female ability the overriding environment. In my last year of high school and my first two years of college, as I slowly moved toward coming out as a Jew and as a lesbian, I soaked myself in *Julia* as in astringent, forcing to the surface the ephemera of denial. Each time I saw the movie I wrote in my journal "I am once again saturated!"—a verb that *Webster's Dictionary*, interestingly, defines as "to impregnate fully." No disagreement there—I wanted to have Vanessa Redgrave's baby.

Jane Fonda and Vanessa Redgrave themselves declared to the press that *Julia* had no "aberrant" overtones, but we who read the original short story in *Pentimento* knew the real score. Hellman had carefully written, in a paragraph never incorporated into the film's narration, "In those years, and the years after Julia's death, I have had plenty of time to think about the love I had for her, too strong and too complicated to be defined as only the sexual yearnings of one girl for another. And yet certainly that was there."

It was this passage that sent me back to the Circle Theater and the Biograph time and again, to saturate myself in the scene where Hellman and Julia have their historic camp out. The short story suggests that this trip took place when the two women were close to age seventeen or eighteen, just my age then, as I sat spellbound in the theater; but of course Jane Fonda and Vanessa Redgrave were in their late thirties at least, and playing at being in their young twenties for that scene. The blurriness of age worked for me: it suggested that one could love another woman as an adolescent and in one's twenties, one's thirties; the cumulative power of age only polishing the sheen on the spoken declaration of love.

"I love you, Julia," says Lillian Hellman. In the film, Julia says nothing and does nothing in response, merely permitting the radiant Hellman to snuggle into her arms; but in the original story, Hellman wrote "She stared at me and took my hand to her face." Simply knowing, when I was eighteen, that Hellman and Julia had lived these moments at eighteen themselves, made possible a world ahead of risk and woman-loving. And yet, the Hollywood film *Julia* denied this might be so.

Later we move on to see an adult Hellman mocked for her friend's politics. Julia, as an heiress who elected to give her money to antifascist work, was evidently quite a laughingstock in certain New York society circles, and Hellman endured this social hostility vicariously. Without question, the real Lillian Hellman—who, when called before Joseph McCarthy's House Un-American Activities Committee declared "I will not cut my conscience to fit this year's fashions," and rather than naming names was blacklisted for years—did indeed challenge those who maligned her beloved friends. But what we see on-screen in the movie is a drunken young man, Sammy, hinting that Hellman and Julia have been adolescent lovers. "The whole world knows about you and Julia," he leers, and Jane Fonda, as Hellman, slaps his face so hard he falls backward, and she overturns the table and walks out.

This scene is powerful enough to have many interpretations. But at seventeen, the message I got was loud and clear: how dare anyone imply that women's love for one another might contain an element of physical passion and desire! Though Sammy has just confessed to an incestuous relationship with his sister, in this same scene, it is Hellman and Julia who would be sullied by sexual innuendo. These terrific women are too politically noble to experiment with sex—although their various male partners win approval in the movie, and Julia has a baby out of wedlock. No, what is unthinkable is that female relationships might have sexual overtones, particularly in those war years when so many men were gone (and relying on women's fidelity).

I reflected on this logic, as a pimply, hormonal teenager in the dark. Every film I'd seen where a woman slapped a man or otherwise knocked him silly made clear that this was permissable if he had been "fresh," and I wondered if I would ever be called upon to punch somebody out. I had been slapped across the face myself on two unpleasant occasions, and couldn't imagine gathering the force in my writing hand to inflict this humiliating gesture on another person. But what truly worried me was hearing movie audience after movie audience cheer as Jane Fonda slapped the gentleman who lesbian-baited her. Which was the more feminist response? Cheering excitedly for a woman throwing a punch? Or keen disappointment with the homophobic motive behind that right hook? If someone asked me if I'd ever had sexual feelings for other girls, was it politically upright and noble to respond with my fists? Why was the hint of lesbianism the taunt that would not stand?

I never once forgot that the movie was about Lillian Hellman, a Jewish woman writer and a role model for me, who had survived years of no work after McCarthy banned her from employment as a playwright. I felt, in the slap delivered by Jane Fonda, all of Hellman's rage that the innuendos of smug men—like Joseph McCarthy and his minions—were all it took to silence women's writing, women's credibility as political agents. To survive a trip through Nazi Germany on behalf of imprisoned

Jews and then be blacklisted in America as suspect, enemy, corrupt—this too was weighing on Hellman's pen when she wrote "Julia" as a short story. Perhaps, I reasoned, the slap in the face was a warning to all men who have no other interest than creating a tabloid reputation for women awakening to their own power. And yet audiences everywhere went home reminded that to call a strong woman a lesbian is the ultimate insult, to be answered with violence.

But at eighteen, I waited in vain to be called a lesbian by a man who believed this would insult me, if only so that I could reply "Yes, I am, and loving it," or "Are you the alternative?" or any of the other clever replies I had read about in feminist periodicals. I waited in vain to be asked to carry hidden supplies or money across enemy lines to fight the good fight for this cause or that. I waited in vain to meet a woman I could hold at a campfire and openly love.

When, confused and irritable, I finally re-read Hellman's short story to see if she really had slapped Sammy's face, I was surprised by what I found.

> He said he rather liked his sister Anne-Marie, because he had slept with her when she was sixteen and he was eighteen. Then, perhaps because I made a sound, he said who the hell was I to talk, everybody knew about Julia and me.
>
> It is one of the strange American changes in custom that the drunks of my day often hit each other, but never in the kind of bar fight that so often happens now with knives. . . . And so, at that minute at the table at Small's, there seemed to me nothing odd about what I did. I leaned across the table, slapped Sammy in the face, got up, turned over the table, and went home.

How different was this, the original version, from the movie's homophobic scene! In real life, Lillian Hellman took a whack at

Sammy for comparing her romantic friendship to his incestuous knowledge of his sister. Yet in the film, Sammy speaks invented lines that are nowhere in Hellman's story; Sammy in the film declares that it was his sister who initiated their sexual relationship. "My little sister gave me a look, she gave me a tender touch, and within minutes. . . ." Watching those scenes, audiences might believe that real women do not suffer being called lesbians, but willingly suffer, or even initiate, the crime of incest.

Considering the high incidence of incest and sexual abuse in many young women's homes, this inaccurate scene is downright dangerous. And yet it is "authentic" in that some Americans are more offended by lesbian love than by brothers abusing their sisters.

As a teenager I was flabbergasted to confirm that historically, Lillian Hellman did not take issue with being called a lesbian, but with being taunted by a rapist. And no one would learn this unless they read the original short story in *Pentimento*. How many other screenplays twisted the authentic stance of women, as lovers, as heroines, as writers? I was so angry that I risked taking my father to see *Julia*, although I was years away from coming out to him. I wanted him to bear witness to the moviegoing experience, to see if he, too, cheered when Jane Fonda slapped John Glover's face, just so I could challenge his reactions.

But my father did not cheer, was shaken by the depth of Hellman's endurance, by her haunting final line "I am stubborn. I haven't forgotten." My father looked at me afterward and said "God, that's a heavy movie." He looked at me with such new eyes because he was aware that this was my favorite movie, the one I had been seeing over and over; he realized, then, that I wasn't a kid anymore.

I saw *Julia* because I knew I loved women; because I knew that all Jewish women are called upon to use their available resources to fight Nazism in its varying forms; because my own friend

Jennifer had been killed that year, in a car accident, and I was desperate for insights on how one dealt with the loss of a close female friend to a violent and early death. I saw *Julia* because, as film scholar Andrea Staskowski has said, "Film is a public dreaming; and trivial entertainments, like dreams, embody our repressed desires."

I saw *Julia* for the last time at age nineteen, when I was immersed in Judaic studies and reading *Pirkei Avot*. This Talmud selection contains Hillel's famous proverb "If I am not for myself, who will be for me? And if I am only for myself, what am I? And if not now, when?" I was studying that passage when I saw *Julia* again, and I finally heard Julia say to Lillian Hellman, "We can only do today what we can do today, and today you did it for us."

That line is in Hellman's original short story; it is the greatest modern parallel to Hillel's quote that I have found. It is a mantra of feminist action and interdependence. The we in it, of collective action, is also a smaller we of two strong women loving each other across the chaos of the twentieth century. And it meant, for me, the sliding of my Jewish consciousness over my lesbian consciousness in perfect bonding, at long last; which is a lot to be grateful for, from one imperfect movie.

Coming Out at The Rocky Horror Picture Show

I turned eighteen in the middle of a strange sub-
culture called Rocky Horror. It was a moment in
time when the teenagers I knew did not spend their
Saturday nights drinking or smoking dope or looking for fights; instead, we were all down at the Varsity
Theater shouting ritual innuendos and throwing rice
at a transvestite movie icon. Those who lament teen
transgenderphobia today weren't at my high school,
where my then-boyfriend won first prize at the
Halloween screening of *The Rocky Horror Picture
Show* for showing up in his mother's dress and jewelry.

 The Rocky Horror Picture Show offered three terrific opportunities; you were actually invited to talk
back to the screen instead of accepting a passive

audience role; you were enjoined to show creative contempt for restrictive gender codes of behavior and dress; and you were likely to have gay people in the audience, to experience a non-threatening social mixer with gay adults. The picture was superbly successful in bringing together two polarized adolescent groups—punks and queers—as united dramatis personae in an authentic theatrical rite. Never mind that the film customarily ran at midnight, or, for kids under seventeen, presented the usual R-rated hassles. This was a place to toy with the notion that it was more hip to cross-dress than to be square. And cross-dress I did, binding my breasts flat with an Ace bandage and pulling my hair into a male-hippie ponytail and jogging down to the Varsity Theater in male garb, delighting in the freedom to pass.

For full participation in *Rocky Horror* one had to bring the following accoutrements in a paper bag: rice, to throw during Brad and Janet's wedding; a newspaper, which was worn on the head during Janet's rain walk; a flashlight or cigarette lighter to hold up during the song "There's a Light"; toast, to throw when Frank N. Furter proposes "A toast!"; a deck of cards, a bell, and sundry other props used when such objects were mentioned in songs. It was a gleeful enactment of the scavenger hunts we'd all enjoyed in childhood. One's status increased notably with each additional prop brought to the theater and used correctly. And, of course, the props were but one part of intimately knowing the screenplay; real troupers knew every line of dialogue and responded accordingly, with group back talk that was known coast to coast ("ASSHOLE!" "ELBOW SEX!") and also less frequently heard replies ("Magenta, don't let your mind wander; it's too small to go outside by itself").

We who set our minds to memorizing this retinue of foolery were the despair of parents who yearned for the same studious care to be focused on SAT preparation and college applications. Perhaps that was why we so joyfully returned, again and again, to see *Rocky Horror*—our senior school days crammed with preparation for the adult academic world, our parents clutching us close for the last year; and out there—in the urban landscape we'd soon know in college—all the personalities we'd never been allowed to gaze on before; transsexuals, mad scientists. "It's just a movie," we said, proud to justify time spent not on drugs or junk food—just a movie, at the Varsity.

When I first began college in Washington, DC, I was a drama major, and quickly found in the drama department a clique of gay and punk and new wave students. They all had cars and drove to the Key Theater in Georgetown to see *The Rocky Horror Picture Show* every weekend. We competed with one another for the most outlandish costumes, the most cleverly memorized lines, and the most daring skill: to get out of one's seat during the film and lip sync in drag in front of the screen. In the company of such friends, I was very well cared for, and gradually hovered on the verge of coming out.

My parents, ever-game, asked about this cult movie I seemed to dress up for every week. What was all the fuss about? Could they go, too, some time? They still enjoyed dressing up in costume. Why should I have all the fun? Amused by their tolerant inquiries, I agreed to accompany them to a midnight showing of *Rocky Horror* on April 26, 1980. It was a night that changed my life forever.

My movie date with mom and dad wouldn't begin until 11:30, and I expected to spend the afternoon and evening studying for spring semester final exams. I drove my parents' Buick Skylark over to the university dorm where my new friend Angie lived. A fresh drizzle plastered green leaves against her window while we quizzed each other, paced, flipped pages of heavy first-year tomes, compared notes, and, finally, settled into a cozy bitch session about every personality in the drama department.

At six o'clock we realized we were hungry, and drove down to the Roy Rogers at Tenley Circle for milk shakes and fries. Angie spewed on hilariously about the various college men she'd had, was having, wanted to have, had let herself be tied up with in a storage closet, or had given up on entirely because they were gay. Suddenly I thought I might be able to trust this sister, this eighteen-year-old wild thing.

"I think maybe I'm gay," I heard my own voice announce through a mouthful of french fries.

"Wow. Really? Have you done anything?" Angie stared at me with considerable interest. I looked down at the lonely blobs of ketchup on my tray.

She launched into the who-do-you-like parade, mentioning the few bisexual or lesbian students we knew. Did I like that one? Was I attracted to that one?

Mortified by my lack of experience, my poverty of anecdotes, I shrank back into the yellow plastic light generated by the imitation lampshade, curled my feet in their Birkenstocks, chewed the ends of my braids.

"No—nothing—nobody," I finally whispered. "I like Leslie, and I like Gillian, but it's no use and they're straight, and I've never even kissed another girl."

"How long have you been thinking about this—I guess I should say, having feelings?"

"All semester," I admitted. "I mean, um, since around the end of eighth grade actually." I crunched a mouthful of crushed ice between my teeth, hoping it would cover up the grating sound of my thighs, in blue corduroy Levi's, pressing together.

Angie leaned forward to say something, but at that moment, seeing our empty trays, a harried counter worker whisked over to us and said, "Are you ladies through?" It was Saturday night; the place was beginning to fill up with hungry college students and families with crying toddlers. Clearly, Roy Rogers wanted us to leave so another group could have the table.

"Look, let's just go sit in my parents' car," I said.

"Cool. I'd like to keep talking."

In the Roy Rogers parking lot, we had just settled into the Buick and picked up the thread of the conversation again when a car, light beams glaring, pulled in behind us and sat idling with a kind of aggressive patience.

"I think he wants this parking space," said Angie.

"Jesus, they sure move you in and out of here fast! Look, I'm going to go park somewhere else—I'll just drive around the fucking block." I peeled out and turned into the first quiet public driveway I saw, which led into the enormous, empty parking lot of the Home Mortgage Association on Wisconsin Avenue.

Now it was dark; it was the last Saturday night before daylight savings began. Trees edged the silent lot, guarding our sudden privacy. We were alone, fresh spring rain on the steamed-up Buick windows, and Angie was saying, "Have you ever wanted to kiss me?"

"Oh—no, n-no," I stammered, my heart pounding. "I don't mean for this conversation to make you feel like I'm after you."

"You don't think I'm as pretty as Leslie?"

"I—sure I do, yeah I do. I mean that I didn't bring you here to—"

"I feel like someone's waiting to make the first move."

"I—"

Angie picked up my palm and traced her soft fingernails around and around on the back of my hand. I felt both of us trembling. The steering wheel vibrated.

Look at her she is so she is so she is so—

I don't know how to TOUCH her I—

"Will you kiss me?" Angie finally asked, interrupting my free-range chickenhood.

"Yes," I avowed, not moving an iota, feeling her hand caress my hand like a blessing. "I don't know how."

"Oh, it can't be that different from kissing a guy," she smiled, and wrapped her arms around my neck.

Then, the warm rain and her warm mouth and the soft down above our lips and the digital clock on the dashboard flashing 9:30.

"Mmm. OHH," she moaned.

"That wasn't so bad," I managed to say, casual-like.

"It's gentler," decided Angie, "than kissing a guy."

We kissed again. "You're beautiful," she said.

Much later, after more kissing, I suddenly awoke to the stark realization that in a short while I was supposed to take my parents to the movies. At about this same time Angie remembered that she was, in fact, actually heterosexual.

"You'd better take me back now."

"I know."

In silence we drove the long mile back to her dorm at American University. I thought of and bit back many things to say. Next to me, her pretty seashell eyes were closed.

I took her to the front door of McDowell. "Good-bye," she said, and that was the last look, the last word I had from Angie for some time.

Driving home, I took the loop around Westmoreland Circle like a condemned cowgirl, dashing down Massachusetts Avenue without playing my usual game of counting lucky green lights, and composing my face so that my parents would SEE NOTH-ING, SUSPECT NOTHING, when I walked through the rectangle of light at our front door. I mentally went through my usual habits of arriving at home: Turn off car. Turn off lights. Pull out keys. Walk down front steps. Push open front door, say "Hi," hang keys up on hook.

I was in my parents' driveway. I had kissed a woman. We were eighteen, no longer girls, but women. I'd left my girlhood, my girl reel, unwinding all over the front seat of the Buick.

I turned off the ignition; I had kissed a woman. I turned off the lights and pulled out the keys and I had kissed a woman, had a woman's tongue caressing mine, I was down the front steps and I had kissed a woman and the rectangle of light gave way against my fist as I pushed open our front door and I had kissed a woman. I walked into my house, said "Hi," hung the keys up on their hook, and marveled that no one stopped me, no one saw anything different about me. I had kissed a woman.

My parents were in pleasant spirits, preoccuppied with dressing up for our outing to *The Rocky Horror Picture Show*.

"Did you have dinner?" my mother asked from her makeup table. I stood transfixed by the sight of my own face in the mirror. Did it show? I was a real lesbian now. When would the lavender L show up in the middle of my forehead? I inspected my lips closely. They felt tender, but looked like any eighteen-year-old's lips. I turned my jaw this way and that.

"I said, did you get anything to eat?"

"Huh? Oh, yeah, we ate. I mean I went to Roy Rogers with Angie." I disappeared into my room and slammed the door.

For forty minutes I lay on the floor of my room in the dark, playing my Roches albums over and over, and letting my stomach twirl on the image of Angie's mouth.

At 11:20 my father knocked on the door. "We'd better get going, we'll never find a parking place." Numb, I rose and put on my usual *Rocky Horror* gear, collected my props, and climbed into the back seat of the Buick. I could still smell Angie's perfume.

My mother sat down in the front passenger seat that was still shaped from Angie's body. I choked back a scream. "Movie candy!" Mom announced brightly, showing the gummy bears and Hershey chocolate she had secreted inside her purse; my parents never bought movie candy, only popcorn. The smell of Angie dissolved into the sickening sweetness of gummy bears.

"Okay, where are we going again?" asked my father, who lived in a world of his own and often had to be pointed in the correct next direction.

"The Key."

I could barely believe that on this solemn occasion, my formal initiation into the tribe of Sappho, I was not in some nourishing nook reading Adrienne Rich poems but, instead, on the pavement outside the movie theater with my parents—both of them dressed in their old costumes from the sixties California Renaissance Fair. I turned my eyes heavenward in supplication as we joined the usual midnight cult-film throng and pushed inside for seats. Why was I here? I wanted to be alone, to hold myself steady, cradle my body into the new language of sensation.

Not that the Key Theater, in Georgetown, wasn't gay space of a kind. Here my lesbian cousin Shannon (not out herself, then, either) had taken me to see *My Brilliant Career*, a film about a real-life Australian lesbian writer (whose sexual orientation was never mentioned in the film). The Key Theater was where I went to *Rocky Horror* with all my gay and lesbian pals from the drama department. Now I had brought my parents into this gay lair on the very occasion of my own coming out. Perhaps it was indeed an acceptable place to hide while I contemplated what had just happened with Angie. After all, there was no moment of my emotional life that I had not subjected to a nice long bake in the light spill from a movie screen. I let my reel spin out.

Punks were dancing in front of the screen during the warm-up music, which was always the same: "Money (That's What I Want)," played while assorted cartoons ran upside down and backward. "Look at that guy," my mother marveled. "He is dancing like he's mesmerized, hypnotized."

"LIPS!" shrieked several impatient audience punks, wanting the picture to begin.

I saw my beloved gay friend Jim saunter past, wearing a wig, garter belt, lipstick, and fishnet stockings. "Oh, hi, Jim," I said, indicating my parents. "Mom and Dad, this is Jim; he used to go to St. John's Military Academy." Jim, in character, gave us a Frank N. Furter lip curl. My father began to shrink downward into his I-am-invisible pose.

Finally the movie began, and I automatically threw rice and yelled out dialogue with the rest of the throng. Inwardly I was tingling, my mind returning again and again to Angie's mouth and my stomach soaring. Outwardly I felt myself small and possum-like, wedged between my parents as I had always been at movies, but suddenly in possession of a lesbian silhouette they could not see. I was different now; I had done what they had not, in their lives.

What was Angie feeling? What was she thinking? Was she asleep?—here at the movies, it was one in the morning. Already tomorrow; our kiss already yesterday's dream. I thought of the many movies I had seen that spring semester with Angie at my side, the blue light from the screen illuminating her great profile and half-moon eyes; would we ever sit side by side like that again? "Two women, touching, just at the knees, but connected, extending each other like halves of an oyster's shell," the poet Ronna Hammer had written. Would I be Angie's oyster again, or cast off forever to tumble in the surf?

On-screen the cast was singing "Don't dream it—Be it." I would have to go on with this thing, this being a teenage lesbian, whether or not Angie continued kissing me; whether or not any movie reflected this life in all its bittersweet discovery. And sooner or later, I would have to come out to my parents. Maybe the next day, when we set ahead the clocks: fitting imagery; no turning back for me, now. Spring forward. Don't dream it, be it. I started smiling, thinking of Angie calling me beautiful; I kept on smiling, although my parents could not see me, in the dark.

Reel 3

higher education

Myra and Mr. Sulu

Because my mother and father came of age in Hollywood during the golden era of studio movies, and knew various film stars personally, they carried their knowledge of the silver screen around with them like ripe grapes to munch on in fine company.

They were delighted to cultivate my avid interest in moviegoing when I was young; this was an avocation they could support wholeheartedly. In contrast, they tore at their handsome heads with grief over the problem of raising children in the television age.

When I was growing up my parents had very strict rules about television watching. Television was a medium they detested. I almost never saw them sit in front of the set except during a rare spell of illness.

My brother and I were allowed to watch one hour of television per evening, and we had to pay for this hour: one dime per program. Of course, on Saturday mornings we stole extra watching time, and tried to be honest about adding our dimes to the chipped cup behind the television. But we were very well aware that movies were of a higher artistic class than television, and that our parents were spectacularly disinterested in whatever we enjoyed about popular prime time. We regularly went to the movies as a family, and discussed film plots and actors at length over dinner. But my brother and I learned not to tell our parents about anything we had watched on television, unless it was a PBS program.

Because of this impatience with television, my mother did not sit down to watch an original *Star Trek* episode until 1979, when I was eighteen years old and about to begin college. Even on this occasion she busied herself addressing Rosh Hashanah cards, more or less ignoring the television. But as the cast assembled on-screen, my mother's eyes suddenly popped. "My God, it's George," she gasped.

"Heh?" enquired my father, who was slowly becoming a *Star Trek* fan.

"George Takei! That man playing Mr. Sulu—I went to L.A. High with him! I never knew he became an actor."

She settled down, chin in hands, absorbed in encountering Sulu—the *Star Trek* character whom millions of Americans had already met years ago. I ran to get my mother's 1955 L.A. High yearbook, and sure enough, there was George Takei on several different pages, looking neat and modest in a crew cut.

My mother seemed dazed. "We were in cabinet class together, senior year—I was vice president of the girls' senior class, and George was vice president of the boys' class."

"You had a sex-segregated student government?" I responded indignantly. I was already a radical feminist.

"Oh, it gets better," my mother sighed, and began to tell me about the hierarchy of rules at L.A. High in the fifties.

"Girls had to wear skirts that touched the floor when they knelt down, and we couldn't wear dividers—that meant any heavy jewelry, like your boyfriend's school ring on a chain, that hung down between your breasts and gave the appearance of 'dividing' them. These rules, and many more, were enforced by the student government—by George and I, I guess."

I was amused. "So before he policed outer space, Mr. Sulu was policing school etiquette? What was he like, at sixteen?"

A strange look crossed my mother's face. She put down the cards she had been addressing.

"You have to understand," she told me, "that social life at L.A. High and the other high schools, too, revolved around school clubs—clubs you pledged, and had to be selected for by the reigning officers, like sororities and fraternities at college. Everyone who was . . . well . . . popular, you know, was in a club. I was in the Baronettes."

"I was a Cardinal, at Fairfax High," my father put in. "I'm even wearing my Cardinal's club jacket in my last role as a movie extra, in *The Day the Earth Stood Still*."

"But the awful thing about the clubs," my mother continued, "aside from their pretentious names and insipid goals, was the segregation. The clubs were strictly segregated, for Jews or for Gentiles, and you had to pledge accordingly. No Jew could join a Gentile club. Even the high school administration, even the vice principal, enforced this policy. Can you believe that?"

"Yes," I said.

"Well, I was in one of the better Jewish girls' clubs. And your father's sister, Pat, who was so beautiful and was also in the movies, she was in the top Gentile girls' club, Vogue. Also there were clubs for the athletic guys, the jocks, and one or two for the less popular girls . . . but, again, either Jewish or Gentile." My mother stopped.

"So . . ." I prompted.

95

"So, there was nothing for George," my mother said finally. "I mean that he was Asian . . . Japanese. He didn't qualify as Jew or Gentile. I have no idea what the Asian or black students did without clubs, in a social scene ruled by clubs."

"But he was vice president of L.A. High," I recalled, puzzled.

"Oh, you could do student government no matter what your ethnic background was. That part of L.A. High was very democratic, and appealed to me for that reason. That's why I became involved, in fact. I eventually quit my club; I let them down, all those girls, I guess, but I just . . . couldn't play along anymore." She looked at the television. "It was important to me not to be a snob, to talk to different kinds of boys. I think George liked me. He sure was nice. We sat next to each other all year. We were in a school musical together, but I never knew he became an actor later on."

On-screen, George Takei was taking orders from Captain Kirk: "Warp speed, Mr. Sulu."

I held up the newspaper. "Mom, are you aware that *Star Trek* has been on television for years and years, with a huge following, and has now been made into a movie? And that the movie will premiere soon here in Washington, and that several members of the cast, including George, are scheduled to make publicity appearances at Toys-R-Us next week?"

"Really," my mother murmured.

"You've got to go, you know, and say hi to George; he's a star now."

"A television star," my father snorted.

"A movie star," I corrected him.

The line at Toys-R-Us stretched all the way around the store and out into the windswept parking lot. Enormous posters dominated the windows: "Come and Meet the Actual Cast Members of *Star Trek!*"

We were the only adult women not accompanying small children in the line. "I can't believe you talked me into this," my mother complained, shifting her weight as the crowd inched forward.

"You don't have to buy the toy action figures or anything. Just congratulate him on his career." I pushed my mother along.

"He won't remember me, probably. It's been nearly twenty-five years."

"He'll remember you; no one forgets high school."

When we reached the autographing table, almost a full hour later, George Takei took one look at my mother and reached for her hands, crying joyfully "Myra, of course!"

We did not know, then, the full story of George's life. It would not be until 1994 that his autobiography, *To the Stars*, would be published, chronicling his youth as a Japanese American child forced into a U.S. internment camp under World War II's horrific Executive Order 9066. That order, signed by President Roosevelt in February of 1942, declared that all persons of Japanese ancestry, regardless of age, gender, or U.S. citizenship, could be forcibly removed from "sensitive" military areas—quickly interpreted to mean the entire West Coast. A generation of children, American born, citizens of these United States, grew up behind bars in the heat and snow of isolated camps in the Western interior: Colorado, Nevada, Arizona, California's Death Valley. They had committed no crime, were never charged or tried. Like their bewildered and now-destitute parents, these children were incarcerated solely because of their Japanese racial heritage.

Along with actor Noriyuki "Pat" Morita, who later attained fame as the martial arts mentor in the *Karate Kid* movies, George made the journey from unconscionable childhood prison to adult movie stardom, pleasing and entertaining white American audiences who had conveniently forgotten about camps like Manzanar and Tule Lake in our own country.

There was no mention of the Japanese American internment camps in any history textbook I read throughout my twelve years of compulsory education in a variety of very good schools. I had to learn about the camps from the movies, when I was a high school senior: specifically, a movie called *Baby Blue Marine,* which portrays the conflicting feelings of a young recruit as he meets Japanese American teenagers trying to escape from an internment camp. I saw *Baby Blue Marine* with my girlfriend Jane and her parents, and when I expressed horror and outrage—how could this have happened?—why did no one TELL ME?—Jane's mother said reprovingly, "Well now, you have to remember, we were scared, back then."

After the war, the devastated Japanese Americans, once the most affluent ethnic community in the West, returned to their burnt homes and ruined fields and stolen possessions in California, and took up the frayed ends of their former lives.

My mother came of age in this time when interracial and interethnic socializing were still forbidden by law. Even in Los Angeles, considerably removed from the segregated South, schools banned "mixed" clubs and made no club space for students like George. Despite the seeming success of integration in some postwar high schools—like L.A. High, where my mother attended class with Asian, Black, Mexican, and Filipina schoolmates—one could only look, and never touch.

"I thought your mother was the most beautiful girl in school," George told me now.

My mother, who had been a considerable flirt in high school, blushed and was suddenly twenty-five years younger. They touched hands, ignoring the line of wriggling and whining *Star Trek* fans.

What had it been like, for them, having a friendship in high school? My mother, burning inside because the Gentile world closed its doors to her; George, a probational American, no club open to his talents and kindness at all. Had they ever talked about racism in American society, when they were growing up under its mantle?

"Oh, no," my mother said later. "You didn't say anything that was anti-American. We were very patriotic."

Both of them were busily denying racism and anti-Semitism back then, throwing themselves into student leadership work and good citizenship and academic success so that they might pass, be liked, be left in peace. If only they were perfect, perhaps no one would notice that their parents were immigrants. If only they did everything right, perhaps there would be no more punishment—the concentration camps George had experienced in America; the ones in Europe where my mother's remaining kinfolk died in smoke.

How hard they had each worked to fit in! In their old yearbooks their clothes and grooming are carefully calculated to suit the current rules—which they, as school officers, enforced. As senior board officers, they had the only government power they would ever enjoy, when they were seventeen. George could govern at school, even though he had been stripped of citizenship rights not ten years before; my mother could enforce codes at school, even though countless American codes, such as the real estate restrictive covenants, prevented Jews from buying or renting homes—or from staying at certain hotels or beaches, from getting into Harvard.

But they never talked about those things back then. It took a movie, George's role in a Hollywood fantasy, to bring them back together in the present, where they could talk about reality.

That night, my mother and George talked on the phone, recalling all the pain and glory of their high school days.

I also spoke on the phone with George. "I thought your mother was so glorious," he sighed. "So beautiful."

That fall I changed my major from drama to Jewish history. And I eventually became a lecturer on the history of the American internment camps.

If there is any parallel between my world and that of my mother and her peers, it is that I went through high school knowing I too belonged to a forbidden minority group—the gay and lesbian tribe—and I, too, rarely dared talk about my own "minority" status. I, too, worked hard to do everything right, thinking my academic performance could always get me off the hook if my life was lived just this side of risqué. While I was in college, the threat of AIDS came to America, and I heard politicians from my beloved home state, California, suggest that the old internment camps be reopened as quarantine centers for people with AIDS. I learned then that many of these camps had never been dismantled; one had been used to hold radical demonstrators during the sixties. There were plenty of good Americans who were ready to see the camps reopened, in the eighties, for the internment of gays.

I came out to my mother.

Throughout the years I attended college in Washington, DC, I lived at home with my parents, and in the evenings we watched *Star Trek* together. We saw every *Star Trek* movie, referring to each one in turn as "George's Movie." Warp speed, Mr. Sulu; we who were also different in high school salute you in your journey to the stars.

Another Night at the Tammuz

We wait to be discovered.

This is the ripe plum kept dangling just beyond arm's reach, the notion that if we are in the right place at the right time, a director will come along and notice us and cast us in the groundbreaking movie from whence spills fame. "You—you're perfect, just what I've been searching for!" the director will cry, altering forevermore our small-town status and bankbooks. How many girls secretly cherish this hope, subverting all other ambition to the desperate fantasy of accidental stardom? After all, it happened to Shelly Duvall. And, truly, it happened to me.

I was "discovered" in a war zone.

1

At twenty I found myself in the desert winds of Middle Eastern politics as an overseas exchange student, on a scholarship to Israel's Tel Aviv University for my junior year of college. I was one of exactly two lesbians in the Overseas Program, the other being, by a fantastic stroke of good fortune, my assigned Brazilian roommate. I enrolled in an ambitious schedule of six academic courses per semester, and of the twelve courses I took that year on Jewish history and Arab culture and the peace process, I never once encountered a woman professor. My own woman-identified world began and ended in the confines of the dormitory suite I shared with Paula, who was also twenty years old and half a world from home.

In that first week my mind and body adjusted to the heat, the chamsin winds, the arrogant soldiers of both sexes with their M-16 weapons jangling on crowded buses, the enraging social stratification which relegated strong Arab women my age to the position of janitors in the university. I fended off the endless sexual harassment of every Israeli male I passed. I walked in circles around the armed fortress that was my school. I looked at the signs on student bulletin boards and tried to find, in the Hebrew and English, any indication of a feminist discussion group.

On my fourth day in Israel I found, instead, a small notice announcing a meeting for all students interested in being in a movie. The movie, Paramount's production about the life of Golda Meir, would eventually air on American television under the title *A Woman Called Golda,* and it starred Ingrid Bergman as the adult Golda and ebullient Judy Davis (fresh from her lead role in *My Brilliant Career*) as Golda in her youth.

I had seen no other activities on campus suggestive of a focus on strong Jewish women, and was instantly excited. The possibility of my own involvement in a historic/feminist drama with two of the most arousing actresses on the planet sent me flying to meet the casting director that evening, before I had even finished unpacking my luggage for the year. I walked into the meeting that night brown from summer, my long hair caught in an unraveling braid, my dyke clothing sensible, if frayed— and when I was halfway into my chair the director rose from his, pointed at me, and exclaimed "She will make the perfect kibbutznik pioneer girl!"

My burbling euphoria, later, was not really about being cast in a movie per se. It was about being typecast as a capable, dykey, salt-of-the-earth kibbutz farm girl, typecast as looking Jewish, after an entire lifetime of being assumed Gentile. For years I had been fighting the unintentionally offensive comments from Jews and non-Jews alike: "You don't look Jewish." "You don't look so bad; you can pass." "If you're Jewish where'd you get that cute nose?" My mother's intermarriage with a WASP surfer/movie extra made me a Jewish girl by law, but a Welsh/Norwegian by face, an ethnic sandwich others bit on daily to test the ingredients for authenticity and tang.

I had arrived in Israel terrified that this racial skepticism would follow me even here, that I would not belong—even as I wrote despairingly in my journal about my ambivalence toward "belonging," if that acceptance situated me in tribal opposition to Palestinian women. But being picked out by the Israeli casting director as a Jewish prototype, as the most idealistic and butch kind of Jewish girl—a kibbutz worker—felt, to me, like earning the mantle of identity I had invisibly worn forever. And I remained grateful that, for once, someone with the power to enforce such stereotypes insisted that I looked Jewish.

I was discovered in a war zone; and in the days that followed my rapture was replaced by bone-wrenching disappointment. For after the preliminary agreement that I would travel to the movie set every Sunday and begin shooting scenes with Judy Davis, the director contacted me and regretfully explained that my temporary student visa forbade working for wages. Of course the film was made in accordance with actors' guild laws and I could not contravene. And so, having been discovered, I was ex post facto forgotten. Years later, I saw the film on television in the United States with everyone else, and gnashed my teeth and pulled my kibbutznik hair.

Crushed, I caught a bus and rode into Tel Aviv proper and went to the movies, and found myself once again in that quirky realm of moviegoer culture. For the rest of the year I went regularly to every theater in Tel Aviv: the Ben-Yehuda, the Paris, the Hod, the Tammuz, the Maxim, the Gat, the Gordon. And the movies in Israel were nothing like the movies in America.

To begin with, the wretched excess and necessity of security concerns even during that hopeful "peace" year of 1981 meant that no person entered a theater without first being searched. One opened one's handbag to the theater guards, and heaven forbid any suspicious object, or embarrassing personal item, rolled upward in the backpack to cause public alarm/mockery/disclosure. Seats were preassigned, as in theater concerts, and nearsighted folk like me had the option of begging "Anee rotsa leshevet korovla," or "I want to sit close up." Then one lurched forward into an inevitably uncomfortable room, for many of the theaters were simply converted civic auditoriums, with folding chairs of the same comfort level as a pinecone. Rarely was a conventional candy counter offered to moviegoers, either; the prudent brought in their own chocolate bars, and in Israel the chocolate—primarily manufactured by a company called Elite—is very, very good. However, the utter lack of air-conditioning in most Tel Aviv theaters meant that one often left a long movie with one's chocolate bar half-melted across one's breasts. I can readily discern, to this day, which T-shirts I wore to the movies in Israel.

I found it peculiar, that first week, that often no one was in the movie theater when the lights dimmed, and I soon learned that this was because the 19:15 screening (7:15 P.M.) actually began with nearly forty minutes of commercials and public service ads. There were no commercials on Israeli television, for the excellent reason that Israel had only one channel, and with the Hebrew news at 6:00, the Arab news at 7:00 and the English news at 8:00 there was barely time for other fine programs (such as Donald Duck cartoons and imported American reruns of *Dallas* and *Rhoda*), let alone advertisements. Thus the only place one saw commercials in Israel was at the movies, and it followed that these were large-scale miniproductions intentionally filmed for the large screen. Ads for the eternally competing banks: Bank Discount, Bank Leumi, and Bank Hapoalim, featured song and dance, men in drag, hip young folk in recording studios, and other distractions. During the day one heard bus drivers and grandmothers humming these bank jingles absent mindedly.

A really popular commercial, which Israeli families came into the movie theater to cheer on, was for a modern refrigerator, filmed in a tantalizing long-range tracking shot as its enormous door slowly opened. Then, extended and gleaming, the refrigerator shelves disgorged a mouthwatering display of every dairy dessert and side dish known to Israel: ten colors of Yowgli-brand yogurt, ten kinds of Danni-brand chocolate pudding, the meltingly wonderful Milky, which was two-thirds pudding and one-third whipped cream; eshel, a watery dairy dish; sour creams, Telma-brand cottage cheeses, and jars of chocolate and hazelnut spread which Israeli children ate on bread after school. This was the full dairy section of the most urban supermarket stock, crammed into one monstrous fridge, filmed three times life size, and every person in the audience—adults and children—sighed "Ohhhhhhh!" in rapturous exhalation at that sight of plenty. I sat among Holocaust survivors and their children and grandchildren; in those audiences the well-filled refrigerator meant security, self-medication, a possibly attainable peace.

Israeli audiences talked back at the movies. They hissed angrily at depictions of child abuse. They babbled excitedly at any American film with depictions of Jewish identity. Almost all the movies were Hollywood exports with Hebrew and Arab subtitles, and thus I was often the only person present struggling to hear the English soundtrack, while all around me the Israelis commented loudly on the film's politics in between reading the titles. Jokes about Israeli politics abounded; one American film scene of downtrodden and sad faces waiting anxiously for bad news drew a derisive shout, "Kupat cholim!" —the name of Israel's socialized medicine plan, long noted for its delays and brusque hospital lobbies.

In Tel Aviv you could see the more intensely macho recent European films—such as *Padre Padrone* or Fellini's *City of Women*, both from Italy—or you could see year-old American movies starring bookwormy Jewish guys (anything with Dustin Hoffman, Richard Dreyfuss, Woody Allen)—or, occasionally, Israeli-made films about commando raids, paratroopers, biblical patriarchs, or other elite men. The litany of screen manliness, European, American Jewish, Israeli sabra, went on ad infinitum and ad nauseum if you were a lonely lesbian exchange student. But just when I had given up on ever finding a woman-identified movie in Tel Aviv, Bette Midler's live concert film *Divine Madness* came to the Paris theater and ran for four months. And for four months, I saw it every Saturday night.

I had not yet come out to my roommate Paula. I knew of no lesbian organizations in Israel at that time (1981). My pent-up internal life of loving women desperately needed an outlet, and so Bette Midler got it all: my joy, my adoration, my open-mouthed lust.

Here was a nice Jewish girl whose entertainment history placed her squarely in the company of queers, even if the Divine Miss M was not queer herself; on-screen, larger than life, laughing at the conventions of female respectability and cheerily teasing her audience with ribald sexual humor, Bette Midler was the perfect antidote to patriarchal action films. Her warm wry face floated reassuringly over the audience. I found her both sexy and vulnerable, maternal and elusive: her rapid characterization switches ranging from languid punk to Broadway brass; her taunting physical casualness, swiftness of sexual poise. I dreamed about her, fantasized about her, sat in the curve of the Paris Theater in a perpetual hunch of desire, cramming Israeli chocolate into my mouth. Alone on my weekly pilgrimage to Bette Midler's face, I could defiantly express love for another woman through my eyes, my body posture, and know that no one in the audience watched me—they were busy watching her, too. I was a Jewish woman lovestruck by the intensity of another Jewish woman and daring to feel this in Israel, where on the streets I was constantly asked why I wasn't out with a man.

Finally, the manager caught me trying to peel off one of the *Divine Madness* posters from the theater wall outside, and ordered me to stay away. Frustrated, I went back to the dormitory at Tel Aviv University and came out to my roommate.

"Hmmm," said Paula. And after a brief silence, she came out to me.

We looked at each other and burst into laughter, and then, as though we had agreed to it already, we pushed our two narrow Tel Aviv University beds together, and climbed in.

2

Paula's performer idol was not Bette Midler but Janis Joplin, whose tortured yowls dovetailed perfectly with Paula's own angry worldview. "You can tell she's lived," Paula informed me as we lay naked beneath my down sleeping bag, letting a Janis tape blast down grittily from our precious tape player. On the tape Janis was snarling "As we learned on the train, tomorrow never comes—it's all the same damn day, man."

It was the Israeli debut of *The Rose*, the movie in which Bette Midler portrays Janis Joplin, which finally pried us out of bed that winter. We could hardly believe the serendipitous happenstance of our two idols melding in one film. Even more titillating were the rumors that *The Rose* included a lesbian scene! Technically, publicists denied that the movie was a fictive parable about Janis Joplin's life, but we knew better: and there was ample evidence that Janis had loved women. One only had to have read "the book."

"The book", as many lesbians know, was an exploitation paperback tell-all entitled *Going Down with Janis,* a lurid sex and drugs exposé "as told by" Janis's best girlfriend Peggy Caserta to some slick and voyeuristic male editors. The opening line set the literary mood of this classic trash: "I was stark naked, stoned out of my mind on heroin, and the girl between my legs giving me head was Janis Joplin." Passed between lesbians throughout the seventies, this text offered proof that Janis had not only liked women, but developed a positive preference for certain sexual positions. I did not own the book, had read it only in installments in my friend Andrea's bathroom; but now there was a movie, ostensibly suggested by Janis's life—possibly with Bette Midler playing out a lesbian scene. It was too good to be true.

In fact, Paula and I were so turned on that we almost didn't go.

Israel, in 1981, was not a land which welcomed a gay or lesbian sensibility. As a dyke I was specifically exempted from Israel's Law of Return, which supposedly gave all Jews the right to immigrate. Paula and I never went out at night as a couple that year, fearful that our body language would give us away as lovers in a culture where we were always on the defensive. Moreover, racism made our occasional errands as a couple unbearable; for inevitably soldiers would approach me (the blondini) with exaggerated compliments and taunt Paula as the ugly one. "Black cow," shouted these boys who were themselves dark-skinned Sephardi; they pushed away Paula's butch Brazilian Jewishness to grab at my blonde hair. "Leave her alone!" Paula would yell as soldiers circled me aggressively; the soldiers always backed off with a parting insult, laughing that I was the beautiful one they wanted and Paula just a nuisance.

I hated it. She hated it. We stopped going out. We went to our separate classes, ran our separate errands, and met at the end of each difficult day, Paula standing on the bed when I came into our room and jumping into my arms, wrapping her legs around my waist and shouting "Kol shelli, kol shelli, minha fofhina," Hebrew-Portuguese words of love and recognition. We stayed in every night and talked about the politics of racism, about our power relationships as North and South American women, about the unfair intellectual dominance of English speakers. We argued in English, Hebrew, Portuguese, and Spanish. Sometimes she berated me closely until I wept, and always we made love all night long. It was not always easy in our little dorm room at TAU; but comparatively, it was safe.

3

Lesbian scenes in otherwise straight mainstream movies, no matter how hamstrung or vaguely enacted, have a terrible effect on many straight men. They talk, yell, fidget, are moved to acts of petty aggression in the audience, for their masculinity is being challenged—indeed, ignored, on-screen. Later on I would witness this vocal male discomfort at American screenings of *Personal Best* and *Henry & June*. *The Rose*, in Israel in 1981, was no exception.

There is indeed a lesbian scene in *The Rose,* during which Bette Midler, as the Rose, is kissed by her presumably ex-lover Sarah (played by actress Sandra McCabe) while sitting on the edge of a bathtub and having her hair washed. As Paula and I sat rigidly apart in the Tammuz auditorium, our carefully expressionless eyes feasting hungrily on the sight of Bette Midler being kissed by a woman for one minute, a riot broke out in the row behind us. The manager stopped the film in the midst of the notorious "bathroom scene" we had paid our shekels to see, and rushed into the audience to quell the surfeit of angry soldiers unable to contain themselves.

There was no way to go back, rewind, recapture the scene we had dared leave our room to see. The soldiers were pacified and rewarded by having the scene that offended them interrupted and cut short. When the Tammuz manager restarted the film, it was well past the lesbian kiss. We sat in the dark aching with suppressed anger and some fear, as the soldiers breathed chocolate and beer down our hot necks.

At the end of *The Rose* there is a scene where the dying Rose, soon to keel over from a heroin overdose, shows up late for what will be her final concert appearance. She walks on-stage in front of her hometown audience, which cheers her from the stands of a huge stadium. Rose, dazed, stands with outstretched arms before them all and says "I forgive you."

"Crucifixion," said Paula, as we walked home later. "The world did it to her because she broke rules. We too must forgive the world which hates lesbian women."

"Christian symbolism in a Jewish movie theater?" I joked.

Paula didn't laugh. When we got back to our room she went out on the balcony, which overlooked most of Tel Aviv University, and yelled "I forgive you," until I took her in my arms.

Yentl: Women Who Want Something More

So the two girls get married. If you want to know how they get away with the wedding night, you have to rent the video. It's a boy meets girl meets girl story . . . very nineties!

—Barbra Streisand on *Yentl*

I went to see *Yentl* the instant it opened, which was during my first semester of graduate school in fall 1983. I went with a lover who was so blithely unfamiliar with Jewish ritual that I caught her lighting her cigarillo on one of my blazing Shabbos candles as we put on our coats to go see this Jewish movie.

The theater was packed with starry-eyed Jewish lesbians, exchanging self-conscious glances of recognition and eating homemade popcorn with tamari sauce and brewer's yeast. Outside the Uptown Theater, in a frosty glass frame, the movie poster for *Yentl* declared that "In a time when the world of study belonged only to men, there lived a girl who dared to ask . . . why?" Beneath Barbra Streisand's face was the stirring tag line, "NOTHING'S IMPOSSIBLE."

"Jews were commanded to study and learn, but Jewish women were exempted from this commandment because a life of scholarship might interfere with homemaking," I explained to my girlfriend, as the scores of Jewish feminists around us sent up a collective poignant sigh during the first scene in which Barbra dons a tallis, the traditionally male prayer shawl of Judaism. "When a culture which prizes literacy and scholarship above all other achievements spends its first four thousand and eight hundred years denying that intellectual quest to women and girls, you're not going to find too many women scholars on record." I indicated the crowd. "But look at all the grad students and law students and rabbinical students here. My generation of brainy Jewish girls is single-handedly reversing the history of female exclusion from learning."

"Yeah," affirmed a lesbian rabbi next to us, catching the conversation. "And before us, it was a handful of Jewish women who pushed the second wave of feminism across America . . . Betty Friedan, Gloria Steinem, Bella Abzug, Shulamith Firestone; and don't forget the founding mamas of lesbian music— Maxine Feldman, Alix Dobkin . . . Writers. Composers. Artists. Thinkers."

On-screen, Barbra had cut off her hair and put on male-yeshiva-boy drag in order to pursue a lifestyle of Talmudic study in nineteenth century Vilna. "God, she's hot," murmured a young medical school intern seated behind me, who came to the movie wearing a yarmulke and a double woman's symbol in addition to her stethoscope.

"I don't know what the big deal is," said my non-Jewish girlfriend, settling back in her seat and spreading out. "There are an awful lot of boring songs in this movie." I kept my hand on her knee, but in my mind it was Barbra's knee.

All over the theater, Jewish women were laughing, crying, eating, moaning, and transmitting an almost audible radio frequency of what might be called cultural arousal, for this was the moment we had all waited for through years of renting Barbra Streisand movies: Barbra, who during her 1972 concert at the Forum declared she would never have her nose "fixed." Here was the chutzpadik girlchik herself in a story blending the highest of scholarly ambitions with lust and desire, embodying my own personal credo that good brainy talk is indeed arousing, and that study partners do become passionately attracted.

In *Yentl,* Barbra Streisand plays a young Jewish woman in a nineteenth century Eastern European village, whose love of study is fed by her scholarly father, but only behind closed doors. Centuries of rabbinical authorities had declared that women, through their ignorance, defiled higher study and embarrassed the congregation. Men ruled the head and women, with their emotionalism, ruled the heart, incapable of scholarly detachment and objectivity. Women were forbidden to lead prayers in the company of men, to be counted in the minyan prayer quorum of ten, to testify as reliable witnesses in a court of Jewish law, to handle the Torah, to participate in any of the public rituals which defined Jewish manhood.

For a woman who yearned to study in a yeshiva herself,

before the eventual onset of Jewish education for girls, the only alternative was to pass as a man. Yentl follows this inevitable masquerade. The scholarly Yentl changes her name to Anschel when her father dies, cuts off her hair, binds her chest flat, dresses as a Talmud student, and heads off to find a mentor. When she is admitted to a yeshiva she finds a handsome study partner, Avigdor, and falls in love with him. Unfortunately, he's engaged to the lovely Hadass. But through a complicated series of events, Yentl/Anschel ends up marrying Hadass instead, and spends the rest of the movie evading marital sex and figuring out how to come out as a woman to Avigdor.

The homoerotic subtext is as loud as a steamboat whistle and just as humidly lonesome. Yentl's first real love for a man blooms while she is passing as male herself, and the intensity between the two study partners seems natural because, we must assume, there were plenty of passionate friendships between male yeshiva boys then (and now). Although Yentl accustoms herself to passing as male, when she meets Avigdor's fiancée Hadass she realizes that it is Jewish femininity which turns on her macho study partner—the female appearance she herself has jettisoned in order to be admitted to higher learning. Watching Hadass through Avigdor's eyes, Yentl appreciates anew the appeal of Jewish women, singing "No wonder he loves her!" Is the gaze male or female in that scene? Is Yentl's appraisal of Hadass a Jewish boy's appraisal, or a Jewish girl's desire?

It's a delicious maze for a Jewish feminist audience. Here is Barbra playing a girl playing a boy who gets married to a girl, trembling her way on-screen through an interrupted kiss with the gorgeous Amy Irving. Their expected wedding night consummation goes on hold when Yentl cleverly acts as a "sensitive" male, assuring her/his bride that sex isn't important in this marriage, should never be demanded, even on a honeymoon.

Unfortunately, Hadass both likes Yentl/Anschel and has familiarized herself with the Jewish commandment of onah, the right of a wife to complete sexual satisfaction. Her forthright insistence on being properly entertained reveals, to a non-Jewish audience, historic attitudes of a very positive Jewish sexuality, and the actual legal traditions which encouraged regular friskiness within marriage. Few other religions grant women the right to demand superior sexual performance from a husband. Of course, in the film *Yentl*, our cross-dressing heroine Barbra Streisand is reduced to despair as she realizes that her modest bride just can't wait to lose her virginity. How much longer can Yentl's secret be kept? Can Yentl resist the soft allure and, let us face it, Jewish logic of Hadass? Throughout the theater, Jewish fingernails could be heard gripping and ripping the arms of chairs in a frenzy of displaced desire. It sounded like buttons popping.

In the final scene where Yentl reveals her gender to Avigdor, he is horrified. Yentl claims she went through with the sham marriage to Hadass only to be closer to him. But when Yentl tentatively speaks of forging a new, honest life with her Talmud partner, as a woman, Avigdor agrees: with the condition that Yentl stop studying.

Oh, the heartbreak of that moment. The man who has been one-upped in Talmud class all year by his diminutive study partner suddenly forgets her IQ once he sees her breasts. Now he earnestly lectures her on the divine roles of male and female; the emotional landscape that should be woman's only schoolroom, the feminine intuition that should be more satisfying than literacy. As her face crumbles, he shouts "You women know everything without opening a single book! What more do you want?" "More," Yentl says quietly, walking away from love and toward the freedom of permitted reading.

"RIGHT ON, SISTAH!" affirmed someone in front of me in the movie theater, fist raised in the dark.

In the years since I first saw this movie at age twenty-two, I have had plenty of time to reflect on its phenomenal popularity with

Jewish lesbians. Friends of mine in Ithaca started a woman-only study group coyly named Lentl, in an obvious tribute to Streisand's film; in their community, Lentl stands for Lesbians Eating and Torah Learning. Other Jewish women I know still have posters of Barbra and Amy Irving on the refrigerator. Watching the movie on video, preferably among friends who will indulge the temptation to replay the almost-kiss over and over, is a subcultural obsession in some circles.

We consume and worship *Yentl* because as scholarly Jewish girls we have been told all our lives that we have the potential to succeed in college, but that being smart will turn off our future mates. In *Yentl* we see that conflict writ large in our spiritual heritage, when scholarly girls were nothing short of abnormal.

Growing up before Title IX and its promise of truly equal education in America, we had no movie like this, except perhaps *Fiddler on the Roof*, which addressed the right of Jewish women to pick their own husbands. Jewish girls in most Hollywood films of the seventies and eighties, if present at all, came in two varieties: unlovable brassy slobs, rejected by sophisticated men (as in *The Heartbreak Kid),* or spoiled whining princesses, reformed through contempt and hard work (as in *Private Benjamin)*. Or one could be a victim *(The Diary of Anne Frank)*. The context was always framed to point out that Jewish girls weren't sexy, in a medium that trafficked in sexiness as the definition of womanhood. Only Barbra Streisand had bucked this trend, undulating across the screen in her long loose hair throughout films like *What's Up, Doc?* Barbra, born April 24, a Taurus, like me.

In this country Jewish women have been simultaneously defined as unwomanly—pushy, aggressive—and as the ultimate in smotherlove: the too-caring Jewish mother. These stereotypes began in the late nineteenth century, when Eastern European Jews immigrated to America in huge numbers, fleeing pogroms and the Tsarist military conscription of young

Jewish boys. They brought with them sex-role behaviors completely baffling to Protestant America, which looked askance at a rabbinical husband who read while his wife worked. It is true that Jewish women in Eastern European shtetlach were expected to work hard, even to be the family breadwinner so that a husband or son could pursue Talmudic studies. Although they were denied the scholarly opportunities men enjoyed, Jewish women nonetheless had a long history as merchants and bargainers and skilled laborers, dating all the way back to Proverbs 31: "A woman of valor, who can find? For her price is above rubies. . . . She considereth a field and buyeth it."

Thus Jewish women arrived in America with a long tradition of public activism, work, and outspokenness, in a period of American history when no nice woman was supposed to work outside the home or bargain aggressively in public. Economic survival skills that had kept the Jewish family afloat in anti-Semitic Europe, and the quick verbal wit that had been the only means of expression for illiterate women, labeled Jewish women unfeminine in America. There is no Jewish tradition of female passivity; it had to be learned, in this country.

The Jewish girls born to all the immigrant mothers between 1890 and World War II, as first-generation Americans enjoying an excellent free education, inherited the mixed messages of the twentieth century. Do well in school to succeed; but no boy will marry you if you act smart. Free education for women in America meant that my mother, the daughter of a feisty Polish immigrant named Sadie, could win prize after prize in her Los Angeles high school—and upon graduation receive these words of wisdom from her teacher: "You're a girl who's smart enough not to let the boys know it."

I became the unpredicted next generation, the Jewish-identified lesbian daughter of the intermarriage, born craving both love and scholarship. No movie addressed this dilemma when I was growing up. A smart girl, in the movies, had to take her glasses off (becoming vulnerable and dependent, as well as presumably "prettier") before she found love. No one found a smart girl sexy; and it was the suicidal Jewish writer Dorothy Parker who coined the phrase "Men seldom make passes at girls who wear glasses." Charming and lovable Jewish girls in the movies were not permitted to be smart; they had to be blonde airhead characters, like the ones Goldie Hawn portrayed.

But then came *Yentl*, which Barbra Streisand openly regards as her most important project. On the heels of *Victor/Victoria*, *Yentl* reopened the debate about cross-dressing as a vocational necessity for many women worldwide. Ten years later, the publication of Jewish/transgendered author Leslie Feinberg's book *Stone Butch Blues* would stir the "passing" debate again, and now Feinberg has plans for a movie based on her autobiographical novel. How many girls have cast themselves as boys to seek unjustly denied dreams of study, work, or sheer economic survival?

In *Yentl*, we are reminded of what playing the male has meant, historically, in Jewish culture: not a specific physical masculinity, but membership in the learning community. Had I been born in another era I, too, might have cut my hair to follow the secretive path toward literacy. I have the luxury of seeing Yentl's options as history, as fantasy; yet today there are multiple nations and cultures around the world where schooling is still forbidden for girls, where in the name of religious fundamentalism literacy for women is denied. It is happening in India, in Afghanistan, today.

The impossibility of being a learned woman, and even beyond that, a learned woman who is loved—era and ethnicity notwithstanding—is a pain I lived with before and after seeing *Yentl*. It is a pain which begs attention and discussion. So I took one radical step toward generating that discussion, that memory of forbidden literacy: I went to a Chicago tattoo artist and had the first two letters of the Hebrew alphabet permanently emblazoned on my writing arm, flanked by two bold women's symbols. Never again would I write or type a word without engaging the arm muscles to make those symbols ripple across my bicep and dance a feminist hora. The culture of learning, of literacy and wordpower, so wearily denied to so many of my Jewish foremothers, now speaks its alphabet from my very body.

The tattoo artist was unmoved. "It's not about Jewish women's literacy or anything groovy like that right now," he breathed putridly into my face as I sat awaiting the needle. "It's about the skill of a male tattoo artist named Rob."

Can one be a learned woman and be loved?

This elusive thing, this right to knowledge and intellectual conversation—this right to receive and create scholarship—is still a question of gender. I have chosen to have my membership in language, in alphabetic power, in the scholarly world, worn as a sign on my arm, in good Jewish fashion—although according to Orthodox law tattoos are forbidden. We who are uppity Jewish (and non-Jewish) girls, book readers and woman lovers, make such compromises, wanting the right to forge our own interpretations. Because, as Barbra Streisand says so well in *Yentl*, we want more than just women's intuition as our portion.

Sappho Goes Hollywood: How We Looked to American Moviegoers

While I was at graduate school, I joined a lesbian society called Herizon, which served a floating membership of nearly three hundred women in the southern tier of upstate New York. Herizon was unique in being a private social club rather than just a bar, and its board of officers had labored to establish a calendar of quality programming in addition to the customary beer-drinking and pool-playing available to members. Primary attractions, in those years, were the women's music concerts produced at Herizon, featuring well-known or sometimes unknown performers touring the lesbian audience venues. In addition to those wonderfully intimate evenings with performers like Alix Dobkin, Kate Clinton, Deidre McCalla, and Lea DeLaria, Herizon sponsored movie nights throughout the long cold winters. And Herizon numbered among its most influential members several young filmmakers from the university, who often led our discussions.

All of us were united in our hunger, our almost physical ache for moving images that truly reflected our lives. These were the very last years before lesbian feature films became a reality in America, before *Desert Hearts, Go Fish, Bar Girls, The Incredibly True Adventures of Two Girls in Love;* before Vito Russo's critically acclaimed book and video *The Celluloid Closet.* There were exactly three lesbian movies that we knew of (and watched critically, over and over): *Personal Best,* which ends with one young lesbian leaving her partner for a man; *Lianna,* which ends with a newly out woman being dumped and forced to rely on her homophobic friend; and *The Hunger,* which ends with one lesbian vampire destroying another.

More frequently, we were forced to fall back on any movie we could rent that had a remotely feminist theme, that showed uppity women as friends if not clearly as lovers *(Silkwood, The Color Purple, Times Square).* Had it always been like this? Were there ever any positive images of lesbians on-screen? Would we have to forge such images ourselves, out of necessity? Like a lost tribe, we yearned to know our origins, cinematic and otherwise, and spent hours around the bar comparing notes on early role models, favorite movies, favorite actresses. I had come home, at last.

It was therefore an enormous treat when Herizon sponsored an evening with Judy Katz, whose video presentation *Sappho Goes Hollywood* provided some answers to our petulant questions.

Yes, there was an entire legacy of Hollywood films with lesbian themes, from the twenties to the present day. But in accordance with the Hays Code, which in the thirties, forties, and fifties decreed that no acts of "immorality" could be portrayed on-screen without stern consequences for the sinner, most lesbian storylines ended in tragedy—not unlike the cheap paperback novels of the same years, which featured lesbians as oversexed and suicidal.

Judy Katz, a lesbian who had worked in broadcasting since the seventies, began her research into Hollywood lesbian images after encountering a late night rebroadcast of Lillian Hellman's *The Children's Hour* (1962, starring Shirley MacLaine and Audrey Hepburn). Judy recalled having first seen this film as a young girl—"Why had it stuck with me for so long?"—and began videotaping scenes with lesbian content from other televised programs, after her regular hours at the Southern broadcasting station where she worked. Before video rentals of campy Hollywood films became more widely available, making compilations from broadcasting archives was the only method through which Judy could locate significant clips from little-seen movies of the past.

Originally she thought only to create a useful guide list for other lesbian film buffs. Then, after attending gay film critic Vito Russo's initial lecture presentation on male homosexuality in the movies, Judy noted: "It suddenly clicked—how my findings could be presented."

It took her six to eight weeks to put together a two-hour video documentary, composed of clips from over sixty different movies and television episodes from 1914 to 1984—a seventy-year tribute to "the love that dared not speak its name." At home in her living room, Judy taped her own introduction and narration for the video, and completed the endless editing after midnight in her office at work. The result was an astonishing overview of how Hollywood has traditionally portrayed lesbians—as vampires, as predatory sex offenders, as victims of blackmail and suicide and homicide, as "sapphics" who can readily find a cure in the arms of the right man.

Judy eschewed any film footage from actual pornography, with the exception of two soft-core segments *(Emily* and *Bilitis)* ostensibly filmed by male cinematographers with an eye for the male audience "gaze." Otherwise, the possibility of prurient interest in most of the film clips was negligible: over and over, lesbians were portrayed as unattractive, neurotic, fiendish, desperate, criminal, even where this negative pastiche had some humor to it (as in *The Killing of Sister George).*

Judy's chronological view of film history naturally reflected twentieth-century social history as well. Pre-Nazi film productions such as the classic *Maedchen in Uniform,* made before German lesbian director Christa Winslow was murdered in Vichy France, show the more tolerant lesbian sensibilities flourishing in prewar Europe—a stark contrast to moralistic Hays Code releases in the postwar United States, with telltale titles such as *Caged* or *Pit of Loneliness.* Lesbianism featured on-screen in the fifties and early sixties was often a Communist plot, a seduction technique used by foreign agents to corrupt innocent girls. This aspect appears in the James Bond picture *From Russia with Love,* neatly dovetailing homophobia with Cold War sensibilities toward women's proper role.

By the late sixties, the old Hays Code had collapsed because of commercial and free speech pressure, and Hollywood adopted the familar G, GP, R, and X rating system—opening the door for more liberal (and offensive) material in the "relevant" movies of a new generation. Predictably, lesbians fared no better in these radical years, with sixties films such as *The Fox* and *The Killing of Sister George* insisting on misery, degradation, and death as lesbian storylines. With the onset of feminist filmmaking in the seventies, historic drama featuring strong women *(The War Widow, Julia)* cast sympathetic characters as bisexual, but without any definitive statement of gay politics. The subject of blackmail continued to hover in most of the lesbian films of 1978, for example: *Different Story, A*

Question of Love, In the Glitter Palace. Another 1978 film, *The Rose,* presumably symbolized Janis Joplin's life wherein lesbian affairs were one extension of debauchery, and again, a life ends tragically. And in *Manhattan,* Woody Allen's 1979 picture, Meryl Streep plays Allen's lesbian ex-wife in a role symbolizing hostile emasculation.

But happier portraits began to emerge in eighties films like *By Design,* where two lesbians choose to have a child together. Even critic Pauline Kael called that film romantic, and Judy Katz agreed that "I purposely organized my video to leave audiences feeling more optimistic." Although the gender-romp cross-dressing of hit films like *Tootsie* and *Victor/Victoria* were hardly produced with a lesbian audience in mind, they forced American moviegoers to consider the economic limitations of sex roles, much as *Yentl* raised the specter of intellectual sexism. Judy Katz also borrowed from several television series episodes to reveal the gay-tolerant moments in prime-time programs like *Family* and *The Facts of Life.* A hot lesbian subplot from the 1983 storyline of *All My Children* had our Herizon audience roaring.

Judy explained to us that once she had completed her video, she tried to interest HBO in producing it for sale, but they never adopted the project. For Judy herself to obtain all the rights for every jewel-like snippet of film would have been enormously expensive. Ultimately, the video could not be copied and sold, only shown as a touring lecture presentation.

She decided the material had to be made available to lesbian audiences—"I'd rather educate than make money"—and first presented *Sappho Goes Hollywood* in late 1984 in St. Petersburg, Florida. The most distant gig took her to Ventura, California. Although she was unable to interest the Michigan Womyn's Music Festival in her work, Judy arranged for a friend to take her video to another popular festival, the Northeast Women's Music Retreat (NEWMR). There, the video ran off and on in a jam-packed media tent, where I saw it a second (and third, fourth, fifth) time. Where Judy accompanied the video and gave a personal lecture, college audiences, in Knoxville, Tennessee, and at Wayne State in Indiana, often proved to be the most enthusiastic.

To this day, however, Judy remembers that "Herizon was the most spontaneously wonderful reaction I ever had."

At Herizon we sat, on those damned wooden folding chairs, in that narrow room where it was always too cold even in summer, and when the video concluded we exploded with nervous laughter, looking at one another in wonder. For me, it was both thrilling and gut-wrenching to uncover this cache of Hollywood schlock. I had not known. Despite the unintended hilarity of many film scenes, the dramatic violin music swelling when one male confided to another "She's—a Lesbian!" and our general exuberance as a group audience exploring our celluloid anthropology together, there was a lingering sense of horror. This was how straight America had seen us, all these years; this was the menu of lesbian stereotypes, written and directed by men, with actresses warned that "Taking this role could ruin your career!" It certainly didn't "ruin" the likes of Susan Sarandon, Barbara Hershey, Meryl Streep, Susannah York, Shirley MacLaine, Bette Midler, Cher, and other women who did not go on to be typecast as "lesbian" actresses. But with all that talent, that magnificence of womanhood, that Hollywood power, could no one write a loving, honest portrait—of us?

In the hundredfold membership of Herizon were professors, lawyers, musicians, engineers, artists, high school teachers, linguistic technicians, social workers, nurses, sign language interpreters, massage therapists, psychotherapists, funeral directors, swing shift factory laborers; collectively, we were also students, moms, actresses, composers, lovers, and ex-lovers.

There was a definite pecking order, and as one of the youngest members I struggled to prove myself on that spectrum of hierarchy. Merit was based on competence and savvy, not on the giggling ineptitude so often rewarded in straight-girl behavior. Where, in Hollywood, was any acknowledgment of the century of lesbian competence?—the women war workers and WACs, the "spinster" educators and college administrators, the artists whose lives were not tragic but triumphant? "I only put my talent into my writing," Oscar Wilde is rumored to have said; "I put my genius into living." We at Herizon were mostly young, then, in our early twenties and thirties, tasting one another's genius for living, toasting one another's competence and wit. What was it like for us that night, seeing a history of false tribal ugliness, on film?

It was frightening—despite the festive occasion Judy had created for us. We exchanged glances of anger, as well as amusement. "A pizza of Hollywood lesbophobia," said someone. "A parade of lies," said someone else. "Geez, I didn't find myself in any of those film clips," growled a third. "Do people really think we're all like that woman in *The Killing of Sister George,* who forced her femme girlfriend to eat her cigar?"

"Yeah," said the third woman's partner. "The worst I've ever done is make you eat my cooking."

"We've got to do better than this," murmured the academics.

"We are doing better," responded some of the young filmmakers. "The problem is funding and distribution of independent movies by and about women—and the reluctance of universities or theaters to sponsor feminist film festivals."

"It's changing, now, even as we speak," said Judy Katz as she packed her video away. "With films like John Sayles's *Lianna,* for instance, straight audiences get a more sympathetic treatment of a married woman's coming-out process. But Hollywood is a very difficult place for out, lesbian actresses. That's why these roles go to women who are confirmed heterosexuals, who end up being praised or vilified for their skilled characterization of dykes!"

We stayed late to party at the club, congratulating Judy on her hours of meticulous research and bold narration. It was one of the really magic nights at Herizon, when we all looked to each other with mutual love born of mutual honor; for we had seen, in the Hollywood mirror, the beasts we were supposed to be, and we knew, as Hollywood could not, how false that bestiality was. It was a hundred nights like that one and more, at Herizon, that gave us all the impetus to smash that public mirror, to change the public record of our lives.

Stirred up, enraged, restless after seeing *Sappho Goes Hollywood,* we decided to throw our support behind a well-known Hollywood actress who had dared to portray a lesbian character with humor and integrity. The presentation by Judy Katz had united us in seeking to honor a woman who had made it, who had given us creative characters we could like, who was an unabashed feminist. And so we rented a bus and all drove down to Manhattan to see Lily Tomlin onstage in her Broadway hit *Search for Signs of Intelligent Life in the Universe* (written by her partner, Jane Wagner).

When we first wrote to Lily and informed her that all of Herizon was coming down to see her show on Broadway, Lily actually wrote back, instructing: "Use the password HERIZON and you will be warmly welcomed." We had no idea what to expect, but at the end of that wonderful performance in New York, the theater management ushered out everyone in the audience except us. We waited. And then Lily Tomlin came back out to the edge of the stage and held court with Herizon.

We made her an honorary member of the club and presented our newsletter; looking over these materials with a wry eye, Lily responded in approving tones, "I like your activities."

We rode home screaming, clutching our autographed programs. When I sent Lily the photographs I'd taken of our trip, she wrote me a dashing personal card, concluding "Herizon women: I love you ALL," and this sits on my coffee table to this day. Yeah, Hollywood has made many of us look awful. But some of us—like Lily—have talked back.

Inevitably, Herizon folded. As all of us gradually met our personal goals, the club became a victim of its own success. It was a home, for ten years, to a nucleus of extraordinary women, a mothership to us while we finished university degrees, started new careers, found partners, got sober. The club drew its last breath in 1991, when everyone was buying houses and waterbeds and fitness equipment for settled middle age; no one was spending money on liquor or late-night partying anymore. Just before Herizon closed I threw my thirtieth birthday party there, and on that same night a strange man, who could not possibly understand or appreciate our legacy, broke in and stole our hard-won sound system.

Del became a filmmaker and lecturer. Liz became a filmmaker and director. Faith became a media specialist for public television. Deb and I became women's history professors. Roey ran for city council. Andrea completed her M.D. and went to work in women's clinics in Brooklyn. Laurie continued to work in sound production for women's music concerts and festivals, ultimately setting stage microphones for Martina Navratilova at the 1993 March on Washington. Slim sang in a great women's band called the Fallopian Tubes. Ren moved to San Francisco and opened a women's auto maintenance school, later writing a book on auto care. Marguerite became the graphic designer for *Girljock* magazine. Sharon became an accomplished drummer and won a solo in Ubaka Hill's Drumsong Orchestra at the twentieth anniversary of the Michigan Womyn's Music Festival. Sherry began performing a one-woman play, *Phoenix The,* about her life as the hearing daughter of deaf parents. Several couples now have babies.

In every way possible, we spread across the country and put our lives in the public eye, and became the stars of our own movies, so to speak. Living, now, in Washington, DC, assigning my own students to see mainstream films with happy lesbian characters, walking from gay movie to lesbian film festival on my own block, I know fifteen years have passed with swift-moving winds of change. But part of me is still twenty-two and seated on that freezing folding chair, marveling at the company of those women, and watching, in Judy Katz's video, the heritage of contempt we all had to transcend.

Batman: A Few Notes on Looksism

I saw *Batman* in Chico, California, on a hot afternoon when I needed to sulk in the cool air-conditioning of a friendly neighborhood theater. I rode my mountain bike downtown, puffing with rage; past the Oy Vay Cafe, past the student bars, past Annie August's beauty salon with its rusted turn-of-the-century curling irons in the window.

I was a grown-up now, twenty-eight years old, spending the year in Chico for my first full-time appointment as an assistant professor of American history. The majority of my university students were blonde and athletic and conventionally good-looking, and the town itself not only looked like but was a movie set. Chico's famous municipal park, Bidwell, has been used as a background for numerous Hollywood movies, including *Gone with the Wind* and *Robin Hood*.

California's obsession with beauty, with physical perfection and plastic surgery, came back to me in a rush when one of my students, thinking to compliment me, remarked that my nose wasn't that bad for a Jew. It was this association of my ethnic heritage with genetic ugliness that sent me stomping off campus in search of mindless entertainment.

I chose *Batman* that day because I felt rebellious, receptive to violence. I was not allowed to watch the Batman television series while I was growing up, not because my mother believed Dr. Frederick Wertham's homophobic diatribe about the decadence of male superheroes *(Seduction of the Innocents)*, but because she found *Batman* too violent: BIFF! BAM! POW! My mother's best friend, Joan, also forbade us kids to watch the campy television series, calling it "Batass" when we were out of the room. My surreptitious peeks at Eartha Kitt in Cat Woman gear, after school at other kids' houses, had to satisfy my interest in *Batman* back then.

Big-screen *Batman* in 1989, however, turned out to be the wrong movie for anyone seeking diversion from insults about physical appearance. The movie deliberately fed on the audience's fear of ugly people. I sat in the dark groaning in dismay at the association of ugliness with villainy, my mind racing.

As most moviegoers know, *Batman* chronicles the Joker's journey from dapper stud to lunatic, using a plot I remembered from my *Phantom of the Opera* days: the physically scarred or mutilated antihero who becomes a menace to high society after the "uglifying" injury. Introduced to us early in the film as a vain swaggerer who can afford to brush off supermodel Jerry Hall's compliments, the Joker subsequently falls into a vat of toxic waste and emerges with his features burnt into a permanent grin. Both appalled and fascinated by his own transformation, the Joker capitalizes on his frightening appearance and sets about theatrically killing the locals through tainted cosmetics. Gotham City residents are terrified by the prospect of a makeup-induced demise and go to work product-free, a predicament conveyed to the audience when Gotham City television personalities perform on-camera with limp hair and raw faces.

These scenarios make several points simultaneously. One, the fear of and reaction to facial scarring are dramatic phenomena in our looks-conscious society; two, the very medium through which we are advised to buy cosmetic products—television—is itself dependent on excessive "masking" of actors' natural faces. More important in *Batman*, however, is the Joker's behavior. The theme of ugly-person-as-psycho is apparent in countless old films and folk stories; modern variants include the nuclear bomb-worshipping mutants of *Beneath the Planet of the Apes* who personify our social discomfort with arms-race masculinity. But the standard message is that the hideous among us hide, from shame or for self-protection, and through long years of hermitude, isolation, brooding, ostra-cization, and loneliness emerge as cold-blooded or moon-crazed killers, eager to slice up hapless passersby (or beauteous blonde virgins) who remind them of all they have lost.

Literature suggests an alternative: the funny-looking nice guy, romantically bereft but poetic about his fate. Cyrano de Bergerac is the obvious prototype. But there was also the eighties revival of *Beauty and the Beast* as a television series, with a romantic yet repulsive leading man who, seemingly, enjoys no sexual outlet despite his passionate commitment to the leading woman. Beasts frequently become confidantes and best friends to women, who are attracted to the beasts' understanding, sensitive natures. In this analysis the beasts may seem to be metaphors for outcast gay men, nonthreatening to women. Still, both heroic and anti-heroic beasts usually end up alone, at home, further extending the root of the euphemism for ugly, "homely."

While suffering through *Batman* I thought back on the different ways I had seen women portrayed as ugly in the movies. Typically, angry (read: political) women are stereotyped as unattractive, and fat humor abounds. When women are introduced as ugly in screenplays, one can expect acts of scorned-dame vengeance on the next page. My favorite such movie in the early seventies, when I began baby-sitting and could stay up late in strangers' homes watching anything I liked, was *The Girl Most Likely To.*

In this film Stockard Channing portrays the "homely" but intelligent college student who is forced to room with the most popular campus cheerleader. (Channing appears in padded, drab clothing and extra eyebrow hair to signify her lack of appeal, a twist that certainly drives home the American association of female body hair with ugliness.) After months of celibacy, and torment by her perkier peers, Channing has a near-fatal car accident and—surprise!—emerges from plastic surgery as a stunning, buxom beauty. Does she settle into new happiness? Not really. She prefers to hunt down all her old adversaries, male and female, systematically killing them off, while they gasp with their dying breaths "You're Miriam? You?" Despite this film's rather satisfying revenge on sexism/looksism, it once again implies that ugliness leads to madness in one way or another . . . or that the ugly little duckling within will always control the apparently well-adjusted swan.

Like most Americans, I grew up on a steady diet of media messages suggesting that the ideal "look" in u.s. society is white, slender, Northern European, Protestant, able-bodied, hetero, and under thirty. These are of course standards any number of Americans fail to meet. But rather than succumb to our ugliness, which the movies assure us will lead to insanity, we can buy products capable of transforming us into acceptable images. Handsome people—however defined—receive preferential treatment in hiring, housing, service, and recognition of achievement.

These are not new issues. Harry Golden, a writer who championed Jewish culture and black civil rights throughout the fifties, also wrote a less enlightened piece directing men to "Wink at some homely girl." But if sympathy or pity were once considered appropriate responses to the less than glamorous, revolution and direct action now fuel the activism of the harassed. An accepted prejudice in our society, with its spiraling epidemics of anorexia and bulimia, is the ongoing contempt toward fat women; but there are any number of splendid action groups to combat this, from Fat Lip Reader's Theater to the journal *Radiance* to NAAFA (the National Association for the Advancement of Fat Americans).

In the media, the marriage bond between looksism and sexism is so welded that a woman becomes ugly if she defies convention. An unmarried woman becomes an "old maid." On my beloved childhood cartoon program *Scooby Doo,* intelligent Velma is the nasal-voiced ugly girl in a thick sweater and glasses, brilliantly solving all crimes—but lovelier Daphne gets the guy. In the Brazilian film *Dona Flor and Her Two Husbands,* the mother of the recently widowed Dona Flor tells her grieving daughter that she must remarry or she will dry up and go crazy. Lesbians are simply absent from the media for the most part, which permits straight folks to assume that dykes really do look like men and could never be an attractive neighbor, coworker, or their child's second-grade teacher.

As girls we play at ugliness on Halloween, choosing scary costumes which often feature nasty masks. This trend has, unexpectedly, been interrupted in part by fundamentalist Christian parents who seek to block any hint of devils and witches in holiday fun. By adolescence, few girls choose "ugly" costume-party gear, fearing it typecasts them. I learned this lesson when I was first at college and attended a Halloween dance mixer dressed in a flabby witch mask. Every other woman present had on a kittenish, cute costume or hot dominatrix duds. Only I had dared to show up in something unsexy, and so I was a wallflower.

Men often decide what ugliness is and enforce their standards accordingly. Radical women who defy the patriarchy are automatically uglified in media coverage, their every leg hair mentioned. I observed this at a peace demonstration at the Seneca Army Depot in upstate New York in July 1985. On this occasion over seventy-five women, of all ages and backgrounds—mothers, nuns, students, lesbian activists—were arrested for civil disobedience and detained in the depot jail overnight. Still handcuffed, we were put onto inaccurate scales, and loudly assigned body weights vastly out of proportion to our actual sizes: literally made big, and hence threatening, or sexually undesirable, or both, since we were not behaving as "ladies" do. It is worth noting as well that our group of women was divided into two jail cells—one for those deemed ugly/butch and another for the more conventionally pretty/femme, according to the whim of the officers present.

Lumped, for various reasons, into the pretty-girl category, I was subsequently asked out on a date by my arresting officer, who wanted to know why "an attractive woman" like me had been duped into a political alliance with "those other women." My wrists raw from plastic handcuffs, I replied "But, sir, I am those other women."

After we were all released, we compared notes. Every woman arrested was assigned a weight at least ten pounds heavier than her actual size. We wondered if this was because we seemed threatening—or if the tactic was to divert us from the peace process at hand by making us whine in self-hatred, "Oh, my God! Is that scale, like, accurate?"

In the cool darkness of that theater in downtown Chico, I had time to reflect on this history of ugliness and its role in the popularity of *Batman*. The empty laughter from a wind-up box which accompanies the Joker's death extends the metaphor of mirthlessness for those folk whose faces—scarred or simply ethnic—are the punch line of society.

The Joker, though unlovable, remains a powerful figure, an urban threat in *Batman*. As women we are more likely to lose power when others call us dogs, to have our public stature cut down to size by a charge of ugliness. The powerlessness I felt when my Chico State University student told me I wasn't that bad-looking, for a Jew, cannot be described. There were hardly any Jews in Chico; no one had my mother's face.

There will always be charges of ugliness for the woman who defies convention, who supposedly transcends a particularly ethnic beauty to attain normative Hollywood stardom. Fame and glamor cannot prevent such charges, in a nation terrified of difference. Not so long ago, I overheard a Greyhound bus driver boast to the long rows of captive female passengers, "Barbra Streisand is ugly as sin! Put a paper bag over her head, though, and she'd be fit to live with!" Every woman on the bus cringed, suddenly understanding fame as endless public humiliation and rape fantasy. But no one stood up to defend Barbra's face. After all, we depended on the driver to get us home.

A Tribute to Director Maria Maggenti

By now you have heard of it, the scandalous breakthrough film of 1995. If you lived in a big city it came
to an art theater near you. It is the ultimate girl reel,
the story of two teenage lesbians finding each other
in a suburban high school; or, as the title puts it, *The
Incredibly True Adventures of Two Girls in Love.*

At last, after all those years, I found what I was
looking for: a feature film brilliantly written for all
the brainy baby dykes who lived and risked and
dared, who came out as teenagers. Never again will
smart queer girls spend their adolescence thinking
"But there's no film for me, no movie about my
feelings." No matter what power the censors, the
anxious distributors, the paranoid theater managers
of America may exercise, this film is here to stay.

There is in Jewish liturgy the phrase dayenu, meaning "It would have been enough." It would have been enough that *True Adventures* appeared at all, a gift to the universe, a celluloid fist in the air. My life as moviegoer would still have been uplifted: big dayenu! But ah, it's even better than this. The film's director, Maria Maggenti, is my old friend from Western Junior High, someone who knew me as a baby dyke in ninth grade. In many ways that is our school depicted up there on that screen, and those were our struggles to be accepted in suburbia. Something authentic in my life is part of an American movie, at last.

I only found out about *True Adventures* when I opened the pages of *Sojourner*, a Boston feminist newspaper, and read to my astonishment that a brand-new lesbian feature-length film had been written and directed by a woman named Maria Maggenti. I blinked. There was her photograph; this woman had filmed her debut release in something like twenty-one days, intended her movie for nothing less than a mainstream release in theaters across America, and was coming home to the Washington, DC area for a premiere showing the following week. There was no question. This had to be the same Maria I grew up with, who I hadn't seen in years. I eagerly made note of the night her film was coming to a special gay screening in Washington, and then scrambled to find my old junior high yearbook, the one with the picture of Maria and me.

If you knew Maria in 1975, you would never have imagined that twenty years later she would be heralded as the important new director of a breakthrough lesbian film. She was, at twelve and thirteen, the adorable heterosexual girl in our junior high—so hip, stylish, and appealing that all hearts melted as she waltzed down the hall in her white painters' overalls and shiny lip gloss. Much of Maria's bubbliness seemed influenced by her mother, an outgoing, youthful woman whom I personally observed flirting with Maria's ninth-grade boyfriends at one school function.

I soon learned that inwardly, Maria was terrified of not being popular in her new school, and had a determined course of action for winning acceptance and love.

Both Maria and I came to Western as transfer students, unknown, writer-identified, ahead of our peers intellectually, but where I had sullenly accepted a scorned place on the junior high pecking order, Maria refused to hide behind her writing notebook. I cared not one whit about fashion, and dressed in a "style" approximating Camp Fire Girl Butch, but Maria planned her outfits by sketching her entire wardrobe in her own journal and organizing ensembles. "Don't you like clothes and going shopping and trying on outfits?" she demanded one day when I visited her chic Bethesda apartment; "Hell, no," I replied, leaning against the door frame in my cowboy boots and army jacket, cleaning my nails with a jacknife. I wanted to tell Maria, who understood about writing, how much better things had been at my old Quaker school in North Carolina, where I could work at my own pace and be judged by my stories rather than my physical style. But on that day Maria did not quite understand. "Oh," she said, struggling into another pair of painter's pants as I spoke reverently about Carolina Friends School and my creative writing class. "I get it. You were popular there."

I was fascinated by Maria's ability to attain popularity in our junior high without being mean, for our school was fiercely hierarchical and the scary girls at the top of the heap were the sex and dope queens, unforgivingly cruel to everyone else and particularly to smart or eccentric folk like us. Yet Maria, through sheer charm, whizzed through this wall of unfriendliness as easily as a spoon through key lime chiffon, soothing and smoothing sour into sweet. In possibly the greatest moment of cooldom she attained in eighth grade, Maria stood up during our junior high talent show and did "The Bump" with the nastiest dope queen girl while both their boyfriends were onstage playing drums. Some AV techie in the rear of the auditorium had the presence of mind to shine a spotlight on the two girls, dancing uninhibitedly in the middle of the audience. Everyone yelled "Go! Go!" at Maria—not at the nasty dope queen, but at Maria. She had made it, found her way in, won the right to party with the inner core. And I was still on the outside watching, writing in my notebook.

I was on the outside because at fourteen I had become a dyke. I say dyke, as opposed to lesbian, because I assumed the persona and the stance long before I understood sexuality or participated consciously in any sort of sexual encounters with women. The way I dressed, the issues I raised, the normative feminine trends I deliberately eschewed, the feelings I cultivated toward other girls, are all recognizable to me now as dyke wisdom. While my mother pleaded with me to wear makeup, to have my ears pierced, to choose my clothes more carefully, I consistently attended school in the same dirty pair of Levi's and old soccer camp T-shirts. I was a dyke in ninth grade because I deeply loved my best friend Ruthie and would have fought any man who tried to harm her, and in fact her father was beating the shit out of her at home. I learned, at fourteen, that only dykes do the real work of protecting and loving women in trouble, because only dykes are willing to refuse male authority by constructing and living a separate reality. So I learned, and became, with no role model but myself. And as a writer I felt the frustration that there was no acceptable vocabulary for this love.

Maria seemed to understand. All of us went on a school-sponsored camping trip that winter, and Maria watched Ruthie and I raptly walking hand in hand beneath frosty stars, smoked dope with Ruthie and me, stopped asking about the dowdy way Ruthie and I dressed and asked instead if she could write in my notebook. She wrote:

"Is it because we're both writers? Or is it our common ideas? Whatever, I've felt close to you in just the few short minutes we talked. Maybe it was the weekend. It was a beautiful experience that we could share. A warm fuzzy secret between us. Always— not an idle remark—and sincerely, M."

She told me I could call her if I ever wanted to talk. Later she wrote in my journal, "What is the ultimate high? It is knowing you've made a new friend. A glow like fire warms your heart." For weeks, my journal smelled of her great perfume.

In the months which followed the camping trip I found that, remarkably, Ruthie and I had attained a measure of acceptance by the mean sex and dope queens at school. We could walk the halls holding hands and were not taunted. Whether this was because Maria served as a bridge in befriending me, or because word leaked from Maria to the queens that Ruthie and I smoked dope, I was unsure; but my stature with Maria, who was high status herself, granted me the liberty to be a dyke in ninth grade. No one bothered me. Maria knew I was cool; this was enough. When I was not in the woods with Ruthie, my head on her shoulder, carving our names into a tree, I was committing general mischief with Maria, baring my breasts to passing cars, buying the latest forty-fives in Georgetown, going to the movies.

It was not until the end of ninth grade, when yearbooks were circulated, that Maria and I had our final and extraordinary exchanges about the price one pays for being popular. It began when yearbook photographs were taken of school clubs. Maria sought me out and said "I haven't been in anything this year. I need to be in a picture with other people, to feel like I was a part of something. You're the editor of the school newspaper. Please, let me be in the newspaper club photo." Shocked by her vulnerability, I posed her near to me. I'm the one in the bandanna. Maria's in the painter's overalls, not smiling.

When the yearbooks were distributed, we spent the last day of junior high reading what different girls had written to us. I was surprised to find that I was more popular than I had thought, after all. But then I was invited to sign some other kid's yearbook. I flipped to the back: and froze. There on the page was an anonymous girl's inscription: "Have a good summer, and don't turn queer like Bonnie and Ruthie."

It was the beginning of the end of my overt love affair with Ruthie. I felt waters close completely over my head. My mood ring changed color hourly. What was the right thing to do? I found I couldn't look Ruthie in the eye. There was only one way to finish the school year with a "cool" reputation, and that meant boys. Except that I went a step further, prostituting myself with an adult male.

The last junior high dance. May 1976. Gym crowded with eighth and ninth graders, giddy with the freedom of the coming summer. On the stage, a hired band called "The Blue Meanies," four guys in their twenties and thirties who played only Beatles tunes. Ruthie, Maria, and I stood watching the band sell Blue Meanies T-shirts during intermission, and although I had no money I wanted a shirt. Barefoot, seductive, I approached the band and offered to kiss them all in exchange for a free shirt. I thought this might put an end to the talk of my being queer.

The band consulted one another and came back with a counter offer: I could have a free shirt if I went onstage during their next number and French-kissed the drummer (who was outside having a smoke).

I looked at the stage; I looked at Maria; I looked at Ruthie. I looked at the crowd—everybody who was anybody was there; the chaperones were at a blessed minimum; I was assured of graduating; I decided to take the dare. "I'm going to do it," I told Ruthie, and that was the first and only time she kissed me. Because both of us knew that boys were the currency to get through the toll; that our being seen with boys was a survival commodity; that our own cooldom was so far out no one, not even Maria, could grant us the stature of cooldom we'd need to get out of this school alive. And so my partner kissed me, and pushed me toward the stage.

I had never stood on our school stage before, but found the entrance and waited for the band to begin their next number. Then I walked over to the drummer and threw myself onto his face. Chaotic shrieks floated up from the audience. The band stopped playing and then, to my horror, the lead guitarist bawled into the microphone "THIS IS BONNIE, A REAL SWEET LADY, AND SHE'S GONNA KISS OUR MAN."

Everyone turned and looked at us expectantly. There was no way out; this was my last chance to prove I was hip, normal, cool, before any more yearbooks pinned me to the wall. I leaned down and the drummer, perfectly aware that I was fourteen years old, plunged his tongue down my throat while the entire school chanted "Wooooooooooooooo!" signifying that I had passed the test.

Then off the stage, down the steps, into the crowd, and everyone praising me with little grunts of "cool," and an exchange student whispering "Slut!" and the entire eighth grade gasping "Sexy!" and Ruthie nowhere to be found. But Maria pulled me aside.

"Why did you do that? Why?" she asked me, over and over. "I can't believe you. I can't believe you did that." Her disapproval was powerful. She turned to leave the dance.

I walked backstage to get my free T-shirt. The drummer pulled me toward him and reached for my breasts, saying "Do you have a boyfriend? Whatcha waiting for?" I ran from the gym in shame, and Ruthie found me and held my head and called a cab to take me home.

And, just as I had hoped, everything became easy. No one wrote in my yearbook that I was queer. Everyone wrote that I was sexy, meaning heterosexual; and when school let out for summer, and I no longer saw her every day, I let Ruthie slip away from me, and pretended not to know what a shit I had become.

When I went to see Maria's movie I had no idea what she had written, how she had directed. I'd only seen her three times since high school: once in the Hung Jury, a women's bar, then at the DC Gay Pride Rally, and in 1990 at the San Francisco OutWrite Conference (for gay and lesbian writers). I had followed her work as a journalist and activist with ACT-UP in New York, but I hadn't been aware of her decision to enter film school.

I went to her movie curious, mildly jealous of her sudden fame, smilingly aware of the irony that the Washington premiere for *True Adventures* was at the Tenley Circle Theater, where Maria and I had once gone to the movies on a weekend twenty years before.

It wasn't until we were all seated for this special showing that the evening's sponsors announced Maria herself was present and would take questions from the audience later. The film's two main actresses were also in attendance. The audience was chock full of local lesbian and gay celebrities, writers and activists who had served as role models to me years before; now we were all here in the dark at the Tenley, across the street from where I'd experienced my first lesbian kiss as a suburban teenager, to see a film about suburban teenagers' first lesbian kisses.

I felt my entire life swirling around my head, like one of those glow-in-the-dark constellation mobiles from the Nature Company.

My heart was racing. Would this movie be good? Please let it be good. Everyone cheered when Maria's name rolled out in the preliminary credits. All I could think of was what her name had meant in junior high, the cachet of her personality, even at thirteen and fourteen: Maria Maggenti: can't touch dis! Because she was my friend back then, no one had bugged me in those school halls.

146

The movie itself was, of course, excellent. I laughed out loud, rejoicing in the intelligent script. It was during the scene when the more popular and affluent teenager is rejected by her school clique after coming out to them that I began wondering how much of this was autobiographical. I had graduated before Maria; I was a year older; when she was coming out as a high school senior I was coming out as a college freshman, both of us still in Bethesda, and within driving distance of this same movie theater; but I hadn't been around when her lesbian relationship threatened her popularity. I hadn't been around to make sure no one bugged her. What had it felt like, for Maria, choosing love over popularity? She had, with humor and aplomb, saved and savored those sharp feelings—love, discovery, betrayal, choice—all these years; while I'd been publishing my life in stories, Maria was casting hers in scenes.

There it was on-screen. Our suburb, our high school, our choices as young lesbians in Bethesda, Maryland, in the seventies. She had made a movie about events in our lives—more accurately, hers; but I was there, knees up in the dark, witness to this ultimate authenticity.

The instant the film was over (go see it yourself; I certainly won't spoil Maria's plot) Maria sprang up (to thunderous applause) and said "Is there anyone here who went to school with me? For I based so much of this on what I really remembered from this area; my school, my life, the lush geography, the affluence, the Led Zeppelin music we listened to."

I had lunged out of the house that evening with my unwashed hair stuffed under a baseball cap and I had to chuckle as I realized I was once again the unstylish slob, in contrast to Maria's glamor and popularity. Nonetheless I stood up, my heart pattering so fast I was dizzy, squashed Junior Mints slowly melting on my hot wrists. Heads turned.

Her face crinkled into a grin as she recognized me. "Oh, HI!"

147

"How the HELL ARE YA?" I stammered, while the audience laughed.

I pulled my words together, addressing the assembled throng.

"I'd like to pay tribute to Maria as a person. You've all seen her genius as a director, and this film makes a powerful statement about what it's like to risk popularity and reputation in coming out as a lesbian teenager.

"Maria and I went to junior high together; she was a 'popular girl' who remained a friend to me when I was 'different,' and it made all the difference in the world." I started bawling, which I never do at the movies.

Everyone began applauding.

This wasn't just a movie. This was the girl reel of my life.

Can you remember what it felt like, trying to be popular back then? and realizing you loved girls (or boys)? I couldn't jump all those hurdles; I wasn't always honest. But that doesn't matter now. Maria and I grew up popular after all, if popular means, as she wrote in my 1976 yearbook, "I know I'm happy when I can say I love the world and the world loves me." She is the first to make a baby dyke movie with a happy ending; and her perfume still smells wonderful.

Working with Jodie . . . and Working with Jeanette

I can tell people, now, that I'm a part of Hollywood. But Hollywood has always been a part of me.

—Journal entry, November 4, 1996

In the fall of 1996, I spent three days working as an extra in a major Hollywood film. The film was *Contact*, with Jodie Foster in the starring role as a strong-willed scientist.

In the fall of 1996, I spent three days working with Jodie. And how that happened is as good a story as the movie itself.

No lesbian in my generation hasn't iconized Jodie at some point, and I don't mean to speculate gratuitously about her own well-protected private life or sexual orientation. Jodie was simply our tomboy pinup girl from day one in the late sixties and seventies, because she appeared, on television and in Disney films, as the spunky tough kid who defied protective sexism. Every girl in my elementary school had to choose, at some point, to model herself after Jodie Foster or Marcia Brady; these were the oppositional role models TV offered my peer group. I fully identified with Jodie, who punched out boys, talked sense, and never passively acquiesced to adult control. By watching Jodie's camera work—and she was just about a year younger than me, and lived near me in Los Angeles—I learned that not all little girls had to be cutesy and feminine to win roles as heroines, and therefore I was not the reprehensible oddball I had thought. In fact, the Jodies of the world seemed made of far stronger stuff than the Marcias, who worried about torn slips and boys. I chose to put my pint-sized feminism to good use and was a proudly outspoken schoolgirl, just like Jodie.

1

Fast-forward twenty-eight years. Now a thirty-five-year-old writer and women's studies professor, busily working on the first chapters for this very book, I have still not, ever, appeared in a movie myself. On this day, I am rushing to the intro class I teach at Georgetown University. Strong dyke that I grew up to be, I walk so intently I not only arrive on time—I'm ten minutes early. I can relax. On impulse, I buy a cookie and the *Washington Post,* browse through the movie section.

My eye falls upon a tiny paragraph, announcing open call for literally hundreds of extras to work in the new Warner Brothers film being shot on location in Washington. Bob Zemeckis is directing. The story is from late eminent scientist, Carl Sagan. And, oh yes, the star of the film is Jodie.

(If I hadn't been early that day. If I hadn't bought the paper. . . .)

Two days later I am at my first real cattle call in a slick hotel in Virginia, filling out forms for Central Casting. I am dressed to the nines, but no one is looking at me; they just take the paperwork and shoo me along. Am I available this day? That day? That week? Do I have any particular skills or talents? (Um, a Ph.D. . . . basic Hebrew . . . expired lifeguard license. . . .) Do I own any unique costume uniforms or props I might lease? (Those blowdarts I got from the tribal chief in Borneo. My old Camp Fire Girl kerchief. Five-year staff jackets from almost every lesbian festival in America. . . .) There are thousands of hopefuls lined up and jostling; everyone, but me, it seems, is smoking; posing and smoking.

"I've already been cast," says my old college friend Angie (yes, the same Angie I kissed at eighteen). "I knew some people at Central Casting. I'm going to be in the crowd scene at the Lincoln Memorial!" But days go by and my phone does not ring. I resign myself to being weeded out.

Then, one fateful evening, I come home exhausted to find THE CALL on my answering machine. A cheerful voice informs me that I've been selected to play a female naval lieutenant in the party scene. I'll be in three scenes with Jodie. I have won this honor because my measurements fit, exactly, the expensive officer's uniform they have on loan. I'm ordered to report to wardrobe the next day.

That night I run screaming down Connecticut Avenue, my black canvas sneakers pounding the sidewalk. I shout, "Thank you, Goddess," over and over. Then, back home to phone my father. "Dad! I'm going to work with Jodie!"

My father's long-buried, historic persona as a kiddie extra suddenly flares to life. "Expect a lot of waiting around," he advises. "Pay attention. Be ready to take direction at any minute in between sieges of boredom. . . ." He tells me more about his years as a child movie actor during that ten-minute call than I have pried out of him in two decades. He teases me about being a second-generation Hollywood extra. All this is fabulous, until he concludes with, " . . . and always keep your costume neat."

My costume! The entire spectacular grooviness of winning an extra role is predicated on my fitting into a naval uniform. But, like every hopeful female at that cattle call, I'd lied about my weight and waistline! Yes, I am truly five-foot six. In no way, however, do I still weigh one hundred and twenty-nine pounds! Have I blown it? Will I be fired?

Apparently not. When I show up, trembling, for the wardrobe fitting, I do indeed slip into the full dress uniform without ripping it to shreds. A straight skirt falls to the top of dress pumps, complementing a white pearl-buttoned blouse, a short jacket with medals and ribbons, a gold cummerbund sash, black tie, and high, decorated uniform cap. I will be playing a woman of power—not some background bimbo. This exceeds my wildest dreams.

Gay men from wardrobe exclaim over me with delight. "You've made our job so easy," they say. "You have no idea how many women lie about their measurements to get work!"

Then I'm given a woman's naval-regulation haircut by the attending stylist, Audrey. "I do Sandra Bullock's hair," she tells me. "And I did hair for *Apollo 13*. Say, you have a good aura. Why haven't you been in the movies before?"

(Just like Greer Garson, asking my mother why she hadn't made films.)

We extras are given shooting dates and times. The exact locations are so secret we know only to report to the costume warehouse, where we'll take buses to the actual set. True to Hollywood myth, our "night shoot" begins in late afternoon and runs until dawn the next morning. We will sleep all day and film all night, be fed by caterers. I put the coolest outgoing message of my entire adult life on my answering machine— "Hi, I'm not here right now because I'm appearing in a movie with Jodie Foster"—and prepare for three days in November.

2

So what was it like, working on a studio picture with Jodie? As a lesbian feminist professor wearing uncomfortable but glamorous Pentagon drag, my immediate problem was that many other extras thought I was a real officer. To save money on costume fees, Central Casting had recruited a number of actual military personnel. These folks sat on the set reading military news journals, threatening to quit the film if they had to work Sunday and miss church. They eagerly shared right-wing opinions with me, dissing gays in the military, women in leadership roles, peace activists, feminists, Jews. Finally I blurted, "Look, I'm not a real naval lieutenant, get it? I'm just an actress."

I had spent fifteen years working at women's music festivals all over the country, where most of my friends were techies; as a sometime emcee, I knew all about stage work, lights, sound, but what I'd grown accustomed to was a production staff of women. The first thing that struck me about the set of *Contact* was that it was so masculine; everyone barking orders, pushing film equipment, loading cameras, checking sound speed, was a man. Jodie was very much the star, carefully separated from us all until absolutely the last minute; but despite her intense presence (eyes like ice-blue pool balls), the guiding energy was male. When Bob Zemeckis yelled at me "Short-haired girl, get out of there," and burly gaffers snarled "Don't trip on the cable lines, sweetheart," I suddenly realized I hadn't taken orders from any man since I'd left graduate school. To my horror, I found myself talking back to the assistant director. This was how Barbra Streisand got a reputation for being "difficult," I thought.

We stood in place for hours at a time for the perfect shot. Absolute motionlessness, hour upon hour. My feet, in the dress pumps, grew numb, then throbbed with pain. When we had a long break, sometime in the middle of the night, I sat down heavily in one of the few backed chairs available. It turned out to be Jodie Foster's chair. All three nights, during my stolen chunks of free time, I sat there in her chair, writing in my journal.

Journal entry, November 15, 1996:

Midnight. For the record, I am sitting in Jodie Foster's chair. On this chill evening, light radiates over the capital city, electricians bustle about importantly, wheeling dollies, and I am freezing, the novelty of all this quickly wearing thin. I've been at work for twelve hours now. One scene's been printed; I'm due to be in another colder one outside.

Jodie is small-boned and slender, with a triangular face and incredible eyes—we made eye contact, and it was like playing handball against a hard blue wall, for she is working, working. The Big Z (Bob Zemekis) positioned me next to Jodie as "filler," meaning I won't be seen much on-screen, but will spend this great weekend posed beside her. Zemeckis, the assistant director Bruce, and various cameramen have all turned their attention to the problem of my head perilously overlapping Jodie's on film. "Pan! Pull back! One more! Right away!" they screamed. "Do not talk. Do not whisper. No shuffling. Okay, kids? Rolling. Marker!" Later, a frenzied plea from the Central Casting agent: "And would you extras please not eat the party hors d'oeuvres on the table; they've been rotting under the house lights for two days."

Journal entry, November 16, 1996

We worked last night until five A.M. The second scene, though bitterly cold, was far more successful for me. Over and over, I had to get out of a limo and enter the Hotel Washington lobby. Over and over, I walked in just ahead of Jodie. All of us were tired, frozen, and the irked camaraderie held us together in the wee hours; at one point, in pain aplenty from my high-heeled pumps, I turned to Jodie and said "Well, I can no longer feel my feet." She looked down at my costume shoes and gave me a wonderful, sympathetic "Oy!"

Over and over, bounding up the steps, just ahead of Jodie, then turning to exchange exasperated looks with her as, inevitably, we heard "CUT! NO GOOD! RESET!" The front door was like a wind tunnel, and the streets—watered to attain a steamy look—were a twenty-degree paralyzing chill. There were infinite crew folk sturdily outfitted in ski parkas, ski boots, bala-clavas, gloves, thermal underwear, down vests, scarves. Jodie, in her velvet cocktail dress, was carefully walked to and from her mark by an asisstant who wrapped her in a down coat between takes. "Okay, kids. Same energy. Action background. Action crane," roared Zemeckis, and the warm limo I exited repeatedly felt so luxuriant, the raw street so cold.

Finally, we were through. I took a cab home dressed in full regalia. Pajamas, flannel sheets, phone off the hook, blinds drawn, I slept until two P.M. and rose like a real Hollywood night owl mixing a midafternoon protein shake and returning to the set in my makeup and costume. As I walked through my heavily gay Dupont Circle neighborhood to the metro, I'm sure the combination of my naval uniform and the rain-bow freedom rings on my backpack startled many an act-ivist.

This whole anthropological ant farm is keenly interesting to me. Many rude awakenings: despite twenty-five years of feminism, the production hierarchy here confirms that "The Industry" is still basically conservative and male-dominated. Women do makeup, hair, and lint removal for wardrobe; they also do the "childcare" of shepherding the extras around and seeing that we're fed (SAG members eat first). Men do all the directorial and technical work.

I see that I have been utterly spoiled by my years as a production worker in women-only institutions. I've grown accustomed to female leadership, female crews, racial diversity, and a nonsexist, collective style of process—I also know that such "alternative" methods nonetheless produce spectacular artistic standards. Since, as a professor, I boss young men around daily, taking patronizing orders from strange men here is an onslaught of cognitive dissonance.

As I do my job and ponder all this, the papers just happen to be having a field day reviewing the new Barbra Streisand film, *The Mirror Has Two Faces*. Rita Kempley, writing for the *Washington Post*, was not only ageist but anti-Semitic, suggesting that Barbra could have been another Michelle Pfeiffer if she'd taken "a little bit off the tip." Reading the reviews, I see how women directors get no respect. Streisand, for example, is maligned for being a perfectionist: in a man, that would be a virtue. Barbra's new film is also being panned for exploring a theme so many male directors have taken on: the fear of aging. Blake Edwards, Bob Fosse, and others get to depict their own vanity and changes—why not women? While vulnerability is usually lauded in women, even invented by the media for women who seem too accomplished (top athletes, say), Barbra's vulnerability is tagged as self-indulgent.

No wonder Jodie has that haunted, determined look in her eyes. Meanwhile, the rampant conservatism and competitiveness of the other extras amazes me. Many of the women extras are would-be models, who can't figure out why I'm here. One told me about her string of commercials, then complained that her book club had voted to read *The Mists of Avalon:* "I'm not a feminist!" One group of snobs keeps reserving seats and tables for themselves during breaks, not deigning to let others eat near them. And these women JOSTLE for favorable positions in front of the camera! One said to me, a little acid dripping down her chin, "Oh, so that's a navy dress uniform? It's so dull I thought you were playing a waiter."

An older woman, who told me she's appeared as an extra in many films since retiring, made a most revealing comment. "When I saw all the young, gorgeous woman at the cattle call, I knew they'd call me. Because they have to have diversity of age groups, don't they?"

Every time I bend down, my gold cummerbund flies apart.

Journal entry, November 17, 1996

All done. That's a wrap, folks.

Last night we filmed two scenes between seven and midnight. First we stood for three hours in party formation while troublesome lights were set. The sheer claustrophobia of remaining frozen, without permission to stretch, for endless takes while Jodie and Matthew came in and out of the ballroom, made the less professional extras restless. The poor assistant directors begged them repeatedly to stop talking. Some seemed unwilling to shut up and take direction—and there were a few unbelievable characters. Three senile old people, a couple, and an eccentric woman who continually babbled about meditation, pushed and shoved to the front more from anxiety about what they were supposed to do than from any star vanity. Others pushed and shoved, trying to get "close-ups" by being in the right place. When I was selected by the assistant director to storm out of the room at a critical moment, with all cameras on me, the pinched model to my left actually tried to wreck my uniform. She ripped three medals from my breast, laughing "I knew they were fake. See?"

I readied myself for my big scene.

Background action. Two beats. Cross to the girl in green. Rolling. Playback. Action. Beeper. Beeper. Background action. Cut. Reset. Over and over, I stormed out of the room.

After each take I stood in a doorway with Jodie, watching the playback. I got to perch beside Bob Zemeckis's chair as we watched the scene. "Good!" he said. "We're just checking the gate. Print!"

"That was real acting!" a kindly veteran extra praised me; but the skinny models made crushing remarks. "No way will that ever end up on-screen." "Only an inch of your head got into that shot." "No one will ever know it was you."

When it was all over, they hustled us off quickly to process our vouchers, then pushed us onto buses, back to the warehouse. We turned in our costumes and, at one A.M., I was forced to beg a ride home. My total earnings: one hundred and seventy-two dollars and fifty-eight cents.

I was too jazzed up to sleep and watched an old movie on cable—the first movie I'd looked at since being in one, myself. There wasn't a hint of artificial manufacture apparent to me, though I should now be hyperaware of how it's all put together like a chemistry experiment. This is the debt of gratitude we all owe to the image makers: they do make it look real.

3

Within four months, I was working on the set of another film, but the contrast could not be greater. My friend Jeanette Buck, whom I have loved since college, was completing film school and had raised the money to shoot a feature film for her master's thesis. This independent lesbian film would be called *Out of Season,* and it tells the story of two lesbians who meet in a Jersey Shore diner and fall in love.

Jeanette had sent me a fundraising letter, indicating her plans. The entire film would be shot on location in Cape May during the month of March 1997. I knew that my spring break fell during this period. I offered myself as a production assistant, loaded my Chevette Scooter, and took off.

All of us stayed in a wonderful old house that also served as the movie set for indoor scenes. At night, we slept on the floors in sleeping bags; during the day, we stowed away our gear and cleared the set. None of us were paid—actresses, actors, crew. We did it for love, and because we believed in the project, though the days were very long and very cold, particularly the scenes filmed at the ocean. It was one of the greatest instant-community experiences of my life.

I saw my beloved college friend bloom like a flower as, daily, she fulfilled her dream of becoming director; she was driven, but there was never a harsh word from her, never a patronizing gesture, never any impatience. Several young men, still in or fresh out of film school, eagerly served on Jeanette's crew, showing only gratitude for the opportunity to work. The assistant director was also a lesbian, and barreled through the house every day shouting "Lock it up!" "Hot set!" "Camera coming in!" "How much tungsten do we have left?" "Where's that Advil?" I was an extra in two scenes, as was (unintentionally) the rear end of my car; but my main job as production assistant was to do everything pesky that had to get done, including shopping for food for the entire house. I loaded cable equipment into the Ryder every day. I picked up the daily bagel order, the prop newspapers, the groceries, the box lunches. I brought coffee for twenty-five people at a time. I washed dishes, set tables, made midnight snacks. There was no budget for anything luxurious, so I began using my own money to buy the crew treats. I carried chocolate in my pockets. One night I had shining bowls of kiddie breakfast cereal and milk waiting for everyone when they came in at midnight.

We had a permit from the city police to film in Cape May and to block off streets when necessary, and this was where the real contrast to "Hollywood" power began; in no way did the more temperamental residents of the town show us the respect they might have accorded Bob Zemeckis (or any other male director). My most horrific task was blocking traffic: unarmed, using only my body or a flashlight, waving cars to alternate routes; a finger to my lips, indicating that a scene was being filmed on this or that corner. Young men intent on racing their cars screamed obscenities at me: "You're not a fucking cop!" Elderly women yelled, too. "How dare you block our way!" Others deliberately turned up their car radios, ostentatiously uncooperative, when we asked them to pass by the set as quietly as possible; some revved their engines, drove over our fragile cable lines, flashed their headlights distractingly in unbelievable toddler-level rebellion. An interested, but unhelpful, local woman brought her very young grandsons over to watch me; she left them in the middle of the road with me, where they imitated my frantic traffic motions, gesturing at oncoming cars—an incredibly dangerous place for children, and I finally had to stop everything and ask grandma to mind the kids.

One March night I was sitting on a folding chair in the middle of blocked-off Main Street, wearing five layers: T-shirt, sweatshirt, hooded plaid flannel, black leather jacket, scarf, baseball cap: and still I could barely feel my fingers. It was then that an insane man actually attempted to run over me with his car. He was so outraged that the street had been blocked off that he was simmering, macaroni-like, ready to boil over with personal offense. I explained that we had a police permit. I explained that he merely had to turn right, here, to reach his neighborhood, that the filming would be over soon, was meanwhile helping his town's economy, and did he want to be an extra in a scene? But it was no good. He leaped out of his car and delivered the most acrimonious, finger-wagging, self-righteous lecture I have ever heard: "You have NO RIGHT to be here! I'm going to City Hall to swear out a complaint!" His frantic wife, inside the car, pulled his sleeve, begging him to calm down.

I stood my ground with classic writer detachment, wondering what my college students would think if they knew how strange men talk to me: no respect for Professor Morris, off-campus. There was no convincing this man that I had any authority, though I was civil, reasonable, pleasant, calm in the face of his mounting accusations. Would he have spoken this way to an older male volunteer, I wondered? What possible harm was a one-block detour to him, that he had to react so abusively? Was it how I was dressed—androgynous, dykey, black leather jacket? Would it have helped to lie, to say to him forcefully, "Sir, I'm a firefighter and we have a live wire down up ahead?" Would he have responded to disaster, to fire and potholes, just not to film students? Why was I too slow to take note of his license plate number? My human roadblock act began to waver, though, when the man got back in his car and started to drive right at me.

For the first time in my entire life, I screamed "Help! HELP ME!"

And the film crew came running. They saw the evil man drive right to the edge of my body, then swerve and take off. I was his "chicken" game, that night; but considering his temperament and his penchant for attacking the wrong person, I wonder if he hasn't come to an ugly end, by now.

My knees were shaking. Everyone hugged me. The caring circle of women.

Later, in my journal: "There are still older white men so used to being on top of the roost, so used to giving orders to women or to nonwhite men, that they expect me to jump when they say jump. They are stunned when I don't accept the role of being cowed and subservient. In a position of authority, I am a reminder that white men are losing control of all that power to boss others around, after centuries of state-sanctioned racism and sexism. And for a certain kind of older man to take orders from any younger woman is, for him, an outrage. Facing down that mean guy, tonight, I was scared, but I also thought of all the people of color who have been threatened and treated patronizingly, by white men. I understood the violence born of rage, humiliation."

That night was an exception. The real story was one of incredible coming together in single-purpose unity. When I brought granola bars or leftover pizza to the oceanfront movie set at two A.M., I was called a saint, a godsend, or, as Jeanette put it, a "goddess-send." I found my nurturing, wifely role seductive indeed. Even when full-body shivering took over and I was a frozen fudgesicle of a woman, I heard myself say in my own mother's voice "Good night, everyone—see you in the morning."

Sleeping was difficult after long night shoots. As warmth gradually returned to our bodies, we tingled painfully and began to reawaken, not relax. Sleeping on the floor, my shins ached, my neck ached, my eyes; for a while I shared an attic floor with a woman volunteer who had to sleep with the light on.

But all this was mere detail. The real story was seeing my friend, the director, kick up her legs and act playful for the first time since I'd known her. Her euphoria could barely be contained by her handsome body and expressive, deep voice. The sight of this strong, sometimes moody woman cutting loose, directing joyfully, and even taking time at the end of each tiring day to hug me, made everything worthwhile. I washed dishes and ran errands with a kind of frenzied admiration, glad to do my part.

Toward the end of my stay in the crew house, I got to be an extra in a long oceanfront boardwalk shot, because I'd brought my rollerblades. I zoomed across the film set, as casual as anything. My lesbian cachet soared a hundredfold with the butch crew gals as I showed off. And oh, the incomparable thrill of hearing Jeanette yell at me, "ACTION!" Not half an hour later, of course, I was back at the house scrubbing toilets, glamour gone. But when I did my daily trek to the Acme grocery store that day, a kid who had watched the film scene recognized me. He said, with wonderful awe, "You're the rollerblader, ar'ncha?"

Nervous about filming the pivotal lovemaking sequence between the two lead actresses, Jeanette banished almost everyone from the set. She said to me, "Bon, everyone has an opinion about how this love scene should go. So?" I responded, "Well, they should look like they're enjoying themselves."

4

Contact came out in July 1997. I saw myself on the big screen. I saw myself in the biggest theater of Washington, DC, the incomparable Uptown, and there I was, naval raincoat and cap, getting out of a limo and walking into a hotel, just behind Jodie's head. You have to know where to look.

Jeanette's film debuted at the Reel Affirmations Gay and Lesbian Film Festival in DC later that fall. She went on to win several awards, including Outstanding Emerging Talent, even before landing a distributor. *Out of Season* opened in New York in June 1999, and has gone to gay and lesbian film festivals in Los Angeles, San Francisco, Australia, Italy, Germany, England, and under the stars at the Michigan Womyn's Music Festival. See it when you can; get it on video; that's me rollerblading across the opening credits. Some people are saying it's the best lesbian love story ever filmed.

I still ask myself how I ended up in two movies in one year. I just happened to pick up the paper the day they ran the cattle call for *Contact*. Some impulse moved my hand. That's the mystical aspect of all of this. With *Out of Season*, the facts are plain: I've stayed in touch with every cool friend that I have, and the old girl network lives. Loyalty and love will get you there. But for the new generation of independent women directors, especially lesbian directors, the old girl network is going to make all the difference in the world. And here, in the brand new century, we are finally starting to see our lives on-screen.

epilogue
a ticket stub

After I saw Maria's movie, and later appeared in a few movies myself, there was one more circle I had to complete.

For too many years I had stayed away from Durham, where I had spent my allowance at the movies weekend after weekend when I was eleven and twelve. I had stayed away precisely because Durham's movie theaters and my own preadolescent freedom in the early seventies were such sacred turf I dared not go back and look.

I lived four and one-half hours' driving distance from Durham during much of the time I was working on these stories, but I conjured every Carolina memory purely from the mental vault without driving south to corroborate what I remembered.

Finally, I went back. I went back to teach at a creative writing camp to twelve-year-old girls at Carolina Friends School, where I had been a twelve-year-old creative writing student myself twenty-plus years ago. I read some of these stories to those girls.

When I wasn't unreeling my own personal girl-child movie to current Friends School students, I was out on Durham's back roads in my beat-up blue car, looking for the past's fairy dust. I found the Yorktown Theater closed, turned into a church called Miracle Life. I found the Center I and II Theaters barely operating, dollar theaters now, fittingly the same price I paid at twelve; I went to a 9:30 show one night during a fierce thunderstorm that sent ecstatic wet frogs leaping all over the roads. The projector broke down immediately and we all sat in the dark for twenty minutes; the seats were the same sticky red I remembered from when my father took me there to see *The Exorcist* in 1974.

The Carolina Theater downtown, where I had seen *American Graffiti* seven times, was also still in business, but had been in a complete uproar for weeks since the management agreed to sponsor a gay film festival. Apparently, Maria's film would not be welcome here. Local Christian activists condemned the gay festival and the theater management, and wrote hot, crispy letters to *The Durham Herald-Sun*. So I rode around Durham reading gay-hating mail in the local papers, but noticed that at least one bookstore in town had a Gay Pride Month display featuring several books I'd contributed to. It was some feeling, coming back to the area and seeing my work in a bookstore window, but of course that was one reason Friends School could hire me; I really did write stuff down and send it out into the world to be published.

I ended my sojourn to Durham at the Pleasant Green Cemetery, lying on my back on my best friend's grave. Jennifer, who went with me every time to see *American Graffiti* when we were twelve, who set me on the path to looking at movie nostalgia as it shapes the next generation, died in a car accident when we were both sixteen. I had not been back to visit her grave since watching her lowered into it on April 11, 1977. Now I curled up in the red clay and clover above Jennifer and felt the earth hum into my spine. I tried to write something profound, soothing to both of us, but succeeded only in spilling fountain pen ink on her white tombstone, which I suppose is as personal a mark for me as is the more traditional Jewish custom of leaving a rock.

I drove out of Durham with red graveyard dirt still ground into my knees, a tombstone rubbing on Friends School stationery in my backpack and a ticket stub from the Center I and II in my pocket. I drove past the closed Yorktown Theater on 15-501, past the closed Northgate Plaza Theaters where I used to be denied entrance at age twelve, past the Carolina Theater where Jennifer and I spent all our money as kids and where my gay money isn't good enough for some folks now; past the Ram Theater in Chapel Hill where I encountered the pederast flasher when I was too young to understand; past all the new multiplex theaters, then showing *Apollo 13* and *Pocahontas* and other "new" versions of American history which still make millions by insisting that smart girls earn glory only as supportive wives to famous men. My girl reel played out differently; yet I also am America; and like Maria says, it's an incredibly true adventure. We're still our best biographers, us girls.